MODELLING
Goods Trains, Goods Sheds and Yards
IN THE STEAM ERA

TERRY BOOKER

THE CROWOOD PRESS

First published in 2015 by
The Crowood Press Ltd
Ramsbury, Marlborough
Wiltshire SN8 2HR

enquiries@crowood.com

www.crowood.com

This impression 2020

British Library Cataloguing-in-Publication Data
A catalogue record for this book is available from the British Library.

ISBN 978 1 78500 068 3

Disclaimer
The author and the publisher do not accept any responsibility in
any manner whatsoever for any error or omission, or any loss,
damage, injury, adverse outcome, or liability of any kind incurred
as a result of the use of any of the information contained in this
book, or reliance upon it. If in doubt about any aspect of railway
modelling skills and techniques, readers are advised to seek
professional advice.

Designed and typeset by Guy Croton Publishing Services,
Tonbridge, Kent

Printed and bound in India by Parksons Graphics

MODELLING

Goods Trains, Goods Sheds and Yards

IN THE STEAM ERA

CONTENTS

PREFACE

In one of my many 'other lives' I spent a fair few hours commentating at air shows, where my equally ageing colleagues and I waxed long and eloquently about the beauty of the Hawker Hunter and vigorously debated the merits of the Spitfire Mk IX against the Focke-Wulf Fw 190 'Butcher Bird'. As we shared our memories of a time half a century before as if they were yesterday, we were totally oblivious of the fact that most of our audience weren't even born then.

Our endeavours to recreate the steam railways of the 1950s may be placed in the same category. For most modellers, apart from us fast-diminishing band of greybeards, that railway is now as remote as the Bristol Boxkite was to the one-time youngsters chatting to one another in the commentary box.

From that confession, you will probably guess that my model-making and lineside observations stretch back to post-war Austerity and the earliest days of British Railways. In modelling terms, it stretches from clockwork 'O' Gauge on the kitchen floor right up to eagerly awaiting the latest announcements from Bachmann and Hornby. Sadly there are no personal time machines to transport today's modellers back to an era when a steam railway was always just a short bike-ride away. Nonetheless I hope that the following chapters will at least provide a few snapshots of what the railways were like and how they operated on a day-to-day basis. Naturally I further hope that this may help your own efforts to create a model that is truly 'railway-like'.

ACKNOWLEDGEMENTS

With a half-century of modelling history fast vanishing behind me, it is no easy task to properly credit all those who have contributed to my endeavours. I dread the thought of waking in the small hours to the realization that I have omitted a key figure.

I must start with my late parents, whose generosity, even in the leanest of times, was unbounded. My dear old dad, Bert Booker, was the village smith, engineer, inventor, countryman and a 'supreme bodger': he could, and always did, manage to make something out of nothing. Above all he encouraged me to observe and remember everything that was going on in that rapidly changing post-war era. Those memories were, and are, the main motivators behind my modelling.

Next in line are two of the great names from the last century: Roye England at Pendon and David Jenkinson. Their sage advice, not to mention their outstanding creations, continues to keep me 'on track'.

Due credit must also go to all the countless publishers, editors, photographers and contributors working in the prototype and model press; their efforts never fail to maintain my fascination for the railways. Thanks also to those companies, suppliers and organizations that have helped in the preparation of this book, notably Dapol, Scalescenes, Freestone, Sankey Scenics, Langley and Model Railway Scenery. Special thanks, too, to the archivists who helped to ensure the presence of the period photographs, particularly Elaine at Swindon, Sophia at NRM, Laurence at GWS and Austin at Pendon.

Last, but really top of the list, comes my family. My wife Joan, for nearly fifty years of tolerance and encouragement; for putting up with family holidays that always – mysteriously – seemed to involve close proximity to a railway; and for accepting the constant spread of model-making detritus across the entire house. Thanks to my two sons, whose childhood Saturdays usually meant several windswept hours waving at trains on Shap Fell. Special thanks to Stephen, whose keyboard skills and endless patience turned hundreds of pages of handwritten scrawl into this book.

INTRODUCTION

LOOKING BACK

At the end of the Second World War, life in the countryside and rural villages had, in many ways, changed little from the early 1930s. Horses worked alongside tractors and most agriculture was still the traditional, family-run, mixed farm. The roads were largely tar and gravel and the steamrollers had yet to give way to the new breed of diesels. Not that it mattered much, as most villages boasted few private cars and saw only infrequent bus services and the occasional delivery vehicle. There was also petrol rationing – trust my dad to invest in his BP pump, albeit the only one for miles around (two cars a day was a 'rush').

The railways, although run-down by six years of war, still ruled supreme. They moved the nation's goods and its people in vast quantities and mostly to time, even if the experience for the passengers was perhaps less enthralling than for the blazer-clad individuals at the lineside, engaged in solitary vigils at country stations or as part of the throng at the end of platforms at the major termini. For us it was an era of great change, great excitement and, especially by today's standards, of great personal freedom. It mattered little whether one arrived by bus, train, tube or bike; once there, as long you behaved yourself, you were free to indulge in your hobby. We witnessed at first hand the disappearance of the once familiar

Challow Station on the old Great Western main line, midway between Didcot and Swindon. This was the author's boyhood haunt in the late 1940s and the 1950s. The Castle is on the down platform and is heading one of the regular 'semi-fasts' heading non-stop to Swindon. AUSTIN ATTEWELL

The early days of British Railways produced an abundance of experimental liveries. Some of these were driven by British Railways' marketing department, while others came from the regions themselves. The former GWR turned out engines with the official style of BRITISH RAILWAYS in a sans serif font, as on this Mogul, but their more prestigious locos had the wording in the old company's style. GREAT WESTERN TRUST

'Big Four' liveries and the advent of the 'new look' British Railways. For many of us the transition from (albeit grimy) green to sparkling, shiny black did not always meet with universal approval. The new official logo was swiftly dubbed 'the Cycling Lion', but in our neck of the woods it became 'the Ferret and Dartboard', perhaps a more suitable reflection of traditional rural pursuits?

Whatever their colour scheme there were certainly plenty of trains to be 'copped'. Expresses thundered through well into 80 mph plus, while lengthy goods trains seemed to plod past on the relief at little more than walking pace. If you were lucky, the local signalman might invite you up into the warmth and highly polished sanctuary of the box. If you were even luckier, and hopped over the fence into the meadow, then a stroll down to the freight held at the inner-home might well be rewarded with a footplate ride back to the far end of the platform. Jumping down from that holy of holies was nothing for village kids used to hopping off moving tractors.

It isn't at all surprising, then, that those long-departed goods trains hold a special place in my archive of memories.

The rest of that world has also vanished beyond recall. No more Eagle or 'Children's Hour'; no more Meccano Magazine or Trains Illustrated. Even the once 'immemorial elms' are now but distant memories. But at least modellers can recreate that vanished era, or at least a part of it, in our own mini-worlds.

I expect those brief snapshots will trigger similar recollections from the older readers of the 'steam generation' and I hope they may also whet the appetites of many younger and would-be modellers who are keen to discover more about those distant days. This book will try to offer some insight into how the railways worked, particularly in respect of its goods traffic. Above all, it will give some pointers about achieving that most elusive quality: atmosphere.

'WE'VE NEVER HAD IT SO GOOD'

In purely physical terms the hobby has never been better served. Manufacturers, from the giants like Hornby and Bachmann down to the smallest cottage-industry suppliers, are producing items to a standard of accuracy quite undreamed of just a few decades ago. These alone, however, do not make for a wholly convincing portrait of the steam railway. They indeed look wonderfully attractive and realistic, at least as models, but no matter how skilful the modeller may be, to just display and run them 'straight from the box' (SFB) will never make for a satisfying representation of the real thing. Accuracy is nothing if atmosphere is absent.

There are already scores of books and guides that will help the beginner to get started in our many-faceted hobby. If one then adds the hundreds of albums and histories that cover the real railway, not to mention all the well-established monthly magazines and countless websites, then the keen modeller is truly spoilt for choice. Nonetheless, despite this plethora of information, no single title or even the most enterprising author could ever hope to cover every aspect of either the prototype or the model. Every reader will have their own particular aspirations, their different skill levels, finances, available space and time – and, of course, their areas of specific interest. It is therefore necessary to establish some early parameters to reveal the aims of the book and its intended core-readership.

TO BEGIN AT THE BEGINNING

This title is one the ever-growing library from The Crowood Press and is a further guide for new or recent entrants to the hobby. That said, even those who already have some experience, more developed skills and an existing layout may still find useful tips towards their future endeavours. Equally, it is hoped that those who are still not fully committed to building their dream layouts will discover some fresh inspiration as well as guidance on how to start and what to buy.

As far as the modelling itself is concerned, the emphasis will be fixed firmly on the most popular scale, usually referred to as OO gauge or 'double O'. This is universally accepted as working to 4mm to the foot (or 1:76 scale). It normally runs on trackwork described as 'code 100' and with a track gauge of 16.5mm. This is the track found in off-the-shelf train sets or available as single items from Hornby and Bachmann. The most famous name in trackwork is

PECO. It is available in pre-curved ready-to-lay form generally known as 'set-track' and comes in various radii supported by a wide choice of points and crossings. This same system is also available in one-yard lengths as 'flexi-track', which can be cut or curved to suit the layout. All these products are compatible and enable the modeller to construct even quite complex track plans easily and reasonably quickly.

There are inevitably some shortcomings with 'code 100' track and with the very concept of OO gauge (for ways to disguise these, see Chapter 4). Nothing, however, can detract from its robust character and its ability to cope with a wide variety of different wheel types. It is often called 'universal' and the operator can safely run ancient Hornby Dublo and Wrenn stock alongside the much finer-wheeled stock currently available. It will even accept most, but not all, scale-wheeled items.

Having determined the main parameters in respect of the model making, we now need to fix the scope of coverage on the prototype. Needless to say we have to place some pretty severe limits on what can be included. Railways have been around for almost two hundred years but there seems to be one period in particular that remains the most popular for the majority of modellers. This is amply demonstrated by the number of layouts featured in the model press and seen on the exhibition circuit. More importantly, it is also the period best supported by the major manufacturers and the many smaller specialist suppliers. It would be misguided to attempt to be too precise over the actual years, but the period from the 1940s to the early 1960s would seem to cover it. This embraces the final years of the 'Big Four' (GWR, LMS, SR and LNER) and the early years of British Railways, leading up to the newer liveries and the dawn of the diesels. The period is often referred to as the 'Golden Years' and stops short of the radical changes recommended by Dr Beeching.

Once the period has been chosen, that still leaves an enormous amount of railway that could be researched and modelled. Setting further limits is a more difficult task. There were seven complete BR regions, each with its own unique character and characteristics; the network was truly nationwide; there were thousands

It isn't surprising that most photographers concentrated their attentions on trains like this. It's an afternoon relief working and is heading for the West Country with the Hall piloting none other than the famous, and fortunately preserved, King George V, best known as 'the one with the bell'.

BEN BROOKSBANK; LICENSED FOR REUSE UNDER THIS CREATIVE COMMONS LICENCE

of stations each served by countless trains of every type and description. But, worthy though all these aspects may be, a line must be drawn somewhere. What is needed is something that would have relevance to every modeller irrespective of their regional loyalties or preferred geographical location. It would also be useful if the focus were on something perhaps less widely covered elsewhere and which could, in turn, throw up a whole range of modelling projects.

The answer, of course, may be found within the very origins of the railways and what would always be their largest source of traffic and revenues: freight. The humble goods train, from fast-fitted vans, lengthy loose-coupled coal wagons and the almost infinite variety of the all-stations 'fly', was the mainstay of the system from Land's End to John O'Groats and from Wales to the Wash. They performed their mundane tasks day-in and day-out and were indeed so commonplace that even the most avid lineside photographer tended to ignore them.

Most, if not all, of the country's railways were originally built for the conveyance of merchandise and raw materials. For Victorian entrepreneurs the very notion of public travel came a poor second to the profits they could make from industry and commerce.

Their intention was to replace the horse-drawn transport on canals and turnpikes with something that was more safe, speedy and reliable. The steam-hauled goods train was the obvious choice.

From the modeller's point of view, the goods train is potentially a far more challenging and interesting proposition than its more glamorous passenger counterpart. A passenger train is just coaches. Although these may vary in number, design and liveries, they are still only coaches. Even the laziest of modellers needs to do little more than open the boxes, add a bit of weathering to the underframes and stick an appropriate locomotive at the front to have a reasonably accurate passenger train ready to go.

Goods workings, if they are to be in any way realistic, require far more thought, research, effort and creativity. The diligent modeller will need to discover more about the various types of train, their purpose, the locos that hauled them and their likely consists (the correct term used to describe the wagons and vans that make up a train).

After an opening chapter describing the tools and techniques that we will be using, later chapters will move on to the various structures and facilities that were the vital interface between the railways and their customers.

AIMING HIGH

The overall aim of the book is to take the modeller, in easy stages, from the shiny new train set right through to the creation of truly railway-like settings in which to operate prototypical goods trains. Those two adjectives will crop up with some frequency as the book unfolds, so a brief discussion of exactly what they mean in model terms is worthwhile.

Authors and modellers can often find it more difficult to explain what they are aiming for than to actually achieve it. Simply relying on words like 'accurate', 'detailed' or 'authentic' somehow fails to capture the essence of the full picture we are trying to present. It goes without saying that all of those are part and parcel of good modelling, but on their own they are rarely enough to convince the viewer. It is more than possible to have accurately scaled models with superb detail and exquisitely executed liveries, suitably posed in an equally well-constructed setting, and yet the scene as a whole still seems to lack an elusive something. It may be an excellent example of modelling skill, but it still fails to capture the essential atmosphere of the real railway. The word 'railway-like' appropriately describes what we are seeking, and so it should since it was coined by the late, great David Jenkinson, one of the finest modellers of my generation.

'Jenks' was not only a master-modeller in EM gauge/4mm scale and in 7mm fine-scale, he was also an able historian, an author and the one-time Education Officer at the National Railway Museum. (On a purely personal note, he was, as Flt Lt Jenkinson, my Maths instructor when I was an officer cadet at RAF South Cerney.) Towards the end of his book Modelling Historic Railways he attempts to explain the elusive factor that can transform a good model railway into something more. David's layouts, like those of many enthusiasts, were largely in imaginary settings, yet they incorporated in superb detail both the trains and the structures that were appropriate to his vision. His definition of 'railway-like' simply required that, 'had the railway existed at this time and in this place, then this is how it would have looked and worked'.

When asked similar questions about my own loft layout 'Wessex Lines' or my exhibition version based on the former Didcot, Newbury and Southampton Junction Railway, I usually describe them as being 'prototypical'. This is now a fairly common term and can embrace everything from the landscape, the period, the various scenes and cameos right through

The early 1950s were renowned for the large number of elderly little engines that had somehow managed to escape the cutter's torch. Three of these ex-MSWJ 2-4-0s spent their last years around the author's home territory; it's natural that a scratch-built example should be a resident on 'Wessex Lines'.

to the trains themselves and the engines at their head. It even includes the speeds at which they run. As an impromptu test of my success, or otherwise, I often challenge viewers to reduce themselves to an inch high and try to imagine they are 'spotting' at the platform end, strolling through the village or helping out on the farms. If they are convinced by the possibilities of this adventure then I have probably got things right and my miniature might-have-been is indeed 'prototypical'. The real accolades, however, are when visitors, unprompted, point to cottages and tell their companions that those were their child-hood homes, or when an elderly gentleman spots a certain loco and tells me that's exactly how he used to sling his cycle on the tender ready for a quick getaway at the end of his shift.

Our aims, irrespective of whether it is a small diorama or a large fully operating layout, should always be to appear 'railway-like' and 'prototypical'.

GETTING STARTED

I hope the following chapters will offer even the newest of modellers some guidance on how these objectives might best be achieved. The hobby should always be fun and the intention is not to resemble a lecture room: if you are still opening the boxes and have never handled a paintbrush or scalpel, there is no need to feel anxious. If the various ideas and techniques appeal to you, then by all means use them, but always remember that it is your railway, your layout and ultimately all your own work.

Railway modelling is the same as any other occupa-tion – the more you put in, the more you will get out. That doesn't just apply to making your own buildings or improving your rolling stock; it applies equally to the tools, methods and materials that you use. Be imaginative and don't be afraid to experiment, as you may hit on an idea that has previously eluded the rest of us. On my various projects I do things no more

This lengthy milk train with fifteen six-wheel tanks, two 'road-rail' tanks and Hawksworth full-brake, and a 'County' in charge, was acquired second-hand at numerous toy fairs about 2005. By early 2015 it had more than doubled in value and was worth close to £400. Even now, though, if you are patient it is still possible to shop around and find bargains.

and no less than 'my way'. After a half-century or so they suit me and I continue to find them (mostly) enjoyable and (usually) satisfactory. I'll be flattered if you take them up and even more flattered if they inspire you to discover your own alternatives.

It is interesting to reflect on the relative costs of railway modelling over the decades. In the last forty years or so the price of ready-to-run (r-t-r) locos has risen from a few pounds to well over a hundred and a basic wagon from under a pound to nearer ten. In that same period, however, the quality on offer has risen to previously undreamed of heights, while relative incomes have risen even higher. Nonetheless our hobby is not, nor ever has been, cheap to run.

I am very conscious of the fact that for many of today's modellers, young or old, that 'tenner' may be just as hard to find as was the spare 'quid' in my day. As I too have frequently had to model on a proverbial shoestring, I have tried to tailor the various projects to a minimal budget. They should be relatively easy to construct and use only a few low-cost tools and simple materials. The kits that are demonstrated are competitively priced and considerable emphasis has been placed on recycling and second-hand purchases. I hope this will encourage everyone at least to make a start: one can always upgrade later as skill levels and/or finances improve. In case you then decide that the hobby is not for you, at least it won't have cost an arm and a leg to find out.

A LAST LOOK BACK

To conclude this introduction I would like to take you back to the halcyon days of steam railways, of Tizer and banana sandwiches, of cheap-day child returns, Billy Bunter at Greyfriars and Dennis the Menace in The Beano. When setting our 'prep', my elderly history tutor at grammar school would always utter the following exhortation: 'Read – Mark – Learn and inwardly digest'. Sixty years later I can do no better than echo his words. Take all the advice you can get from every available source: books, magazines, exhibitions, DVDs and the Web. Study all the methods, materials, techniques and achievements of fellow modellers past and present. But don't just slavishly copy their efforts: 'Never model the model – always model the prototype'.

You are now free to plough through the rest at your leisure. All the projects have been researched, built, photographed and written up specifically for the book. To put it in everyday language, what follows is a step-by-step or blow-by-blow account of model-making from opening the packet to the final positioning and the scenic setting. Where possible I've also tried to include any additional tips from my other modelling activities. It is to be hoped this may help you to avoid the many mistakes that I have made during a lifetime of railway modelling.

This Churchward design, specifically for the fast and heavy overnight freights, was one of the Western's most powerful locomotives. Spotters dubbed them 'Night Owls' as they were rarely seen in daylight. Although they are currently available only as kit-builds on the second-hand market, there is speculation that one may eventually appear as a ready-to-run. GREAT WESTERN TRUST

CHAPTER ONE

MATERIALS AND TOOLS

The model railway hobby has many aspects, each of which will have a varied degree of appeal to its enthusiasts. It is true that the solo modeller engaged upon his or her home or exhibition layout will naturally need to become proficient as a 'designer', 'carpenter', 'electrician' and a bit of an 'engineer' – and that's just to get the baseboards in place. The actual construction and operation of the layout will then demand yet another blend of skills; these embrace the whole package of imagination, planning, budgeting, researching, soldering, and all those ancillary techniques associated with craftwork, artistry and painting. With the ever increasing impact of technology, some understanding of computers and electronics is also fast becoming a near essential. All in all, it's an extensive portfolio of skills and is far removed from that needed when all we had was an O gauge Hornby clockwork train set on the kitchen floor.

It is not the intention of this book, however, to attempt to cover this entire field. We can safely leave most of it to other authors and just concentrate on the enjoyable side of building all those kits and bits that go into making our layouts both attractive and 'railway-like'. Fortunately that means that we will need little in the way of technical wizardry, expensive materials or lavish toolkits. Most of what we do can also be safely carried out on the proverbial kitchen table.

For the benefit of newcomers to the hobby, and perhaps as an 'aide-memoire to more experienced modellers, this opening chapter will take a detailed look at the various materials, finishes and tools, and at the uses to which they can be put. It will also pay due attention to the important question of 'cost'. Our hobby has never been cheap and today's ever-increasing prices and declining disposable incomes have created a problem that shouldn't be over-looked. It is a sad fact that there is a current trend to demand and expect instant gratification. This, of course, is quite achievable even on a model railway, but it always comes at a price. Instant ready-to-site (r-t-s) buildings are available from any high street dealership, providing your budget can stretch to them. The kits and materials on the neighbouring shelves will cost much less and, with the expenditure of more time, effort and some imagination, help to deliver an end product that is probably better and certainly unique.

MATERIALS

CARD

Card comes in an almost infinite variety of sizes, shapes, consistencies and qualities. It is certainly the oldest and most traditional material used by scenic modellers, especially those working in the smaller scales. The exquisite card buildings on John Ahern's 'Madder Valley' showed just what could be achieved with this most simple of media, much of it relying on the recycled packaging of the late 1940s. This iconic layout is now on permanent display at Pendon Museum, who are themselves the most outstanding card-modellers of this generation. Although recycled card is, fortunately, no longer a necessity, it still has its uses and even its own aficionados.

Mounting board

This is probably the most commonly used form of card and is certainly the largest size of sheet that is readily obtainable from most art and hobby shops. It comes as A1 sheets in a variety of colours, all with plain white on the reverse. Some outlets may also offer smaller A3 sheets, albeit at a slightly higher price pro-

Card and paper materials are the mainstays for the kit and scratch-builder. They are easy to obtain and relatively inexpensive; even 'scrap' or recycled items have their uses.

rata. Thicknesses vary according to which brand you buy, but between 1.2mm and 1.5mm appears to be the norm. Most of us tend to use the white side since this accepts pencil, watercolours, pastels, acrylics and even enamels. The black and grey sides, however, do have their uses, especially when employed as a reinforcing material or for internal walls and ceilings. The card, though strong and commendably smooth, is not actually a proper single sheet, but is in fact a series of paper laminations. These can become ragged and separated if poorly cut, and sharp blades and firm pressure are necessary for best results. The laminations can sometimes be an advantage, since the removal of the outer layer leaves a rough inner surface that is textured and more absorbent. This can make excellent stone walls when painted with watercolours. Sheet costs can vary from less than £3 to nearly £5, but it is worth looking out for offers of four for £10. Mounting board is sufficiently robust to be used structurally and unbraced for everything from garden sheds to large barns. It is also well suited to the construction of platforms, docks, bridges and viaducts, and even for roadways and yards, providing they are relatively flat. It will accept brick-papers, embossed plasticard and most fillers or modelling clays, although it is recommended to let all of these dry out under pressure to prevent warping. The A1 sheets are fairly bulky items to handle and it's best to cut off a suitably sized workpiece to fit on your modelling desk.

Recycled card

This can come in all manner of shapes, sizes, thicknesses and quality; the one common factor is that It's free. The best way to approach it is to examine the many sources that arrive on your doorstep or end up in the supermarket trolley, and select the few that appear to have the best potential. Much of it will be too rough or too flimsy for modelling purposes, and even the better materials are only needed in smallish quantities. Store the chosen items in something like an A4 or foolscap envelope, which will keep them together and help you to keep track of how much, or how little, you've accumulated. The most common sources will be the traditional cereal packets and the backs of A4 pads. If you can find any, the small plain pieces sometimes found as internal packaging with chocolates or biscuits are worthwhile additions. The actual thicknesses tend to range between 0.2mm and 0.8mm and all can have their uses. They can be used for complete buildings, but in this role they do need to be laminated and well braced. My own preference is to restrict them to roof templates, garden walls and wooden fences. In particular they are suited to any curved or irregular shapes for which mounting board is too inflexible. Typical examples are curved platform-faces and retaining walls, the undersides of bridges and, of course, the insides of tunnels.

Postcards

These can be purchased in the form of postcards and record cards or you can recycle the non-glossy plain areas of greetings cards. It is also possible to obtain similar material in packs of A4 drawing card sold by most art shops. In general terms this is the thinnest card one can find, but it is also reliable in respect of its quality. It is useful for such detailing jobs as door or window components, quoins and relief brick- or stonework. It is most frequently encountered on tiled roofs, either in strip form or laboriously cut and laid as individual tiles. Most of these cards will take acrylics or watercolours and, once tried, the modeller will quickly discover other jobs for them.

Paper

This can be considered as the very thinnest type of card since its applications clearly fall into that same general area. All paper is described not by its thickness but rather by its weight. This is given in grams per square metre (gsm), and the greater the weight shown then the thicker the paper. The usual weight for copier paper is 80gsm, high-quality writing paper will be over 100gsm, while drawing and art papers will range from around 130gsm to more than 300gsm. At these higher levels, however, we are really talking card by another name.

Paper, in appropriate weights, is always handy stuff to have in one's storage envelopes. In its heavier versions it can be used structurally as a substitute for card, while also providing a high-quality smooth or textured finish. The medium and lower weights will produce roof tiles, albeit better suited to buildings towards the rear of the layout. The very thinnest of papers, such as might be found in the cheaper ranges of business envelopes, can be cut into the correct depth strips and used for roof slates. I would add a note of caution here, though, as in the real world slates are very thin and, at any distance, the rows and individual slates appear as little more than black lines that separate one from the other. A simple painted version may look more realistic than the overlapping strips.

Other types of paper shouldn't be overlooked. 'Roll your own' cigarette papers, for example, make excellent curtains and can be carefully cut into appropriate shapes to hang on the washing line. An even greater degree of scalpel skill can fashion them into garden plants like rhubarb. That just leaves tissue paper, which will often prove useful to form the terrain-skin on the latticework of formers used in the construction of embankments and cuttings. It is also a workbench essential whenever painting is in progress.

WOOD

Here we are not talking about the DIY types needed for baseboard work, but rather the more delicate stuff usually intended for our fellow modellers of aircraft and boats. These woods offer two distinct choices: the softer balsa type and the stronger, more brittle version usually just known as 'hardwood', which may have different origins.

Balsa

Balsa is available in a huge variety of shapes and sizes, ranging from ¼in thick sheets measuring roughly 4 x 36in to the thinnest strips, barely ¹⁄₁₆in square, available in 36in lengths. It is very easy to work. The only tools needed are a scalpel or craft knife and some suitable glue. I use it to reinforce buildings with ¼in square or triangular strips fixed where necessary. Sheet balsa can also be used to form complete inner shells for buildings, clad with thinner grades of card. The thinner strips are invaluable as detailing aids and are perfect for the interior woodwork on barns and timber sheds, especially for the often complex roof trusses. The $^1/_{16}$in strips are very easy to drill and, with a little watercolour weathering and nylon-thread wire, make excellent representations of typical field fences that are past their prime.

Hardwood

When it comes to timber-built sheds and planked fencing, there is nothing that looks more like wood than wood itself. This is where the hardwood version comes into its own. The strips are much thinner than balsa and it is easy to select lengths that can be cut into near-scale planks. Because the wood really is 'hard' I find it easier to discard the scalpel in favour of a pair of side-cutters, or small tin-snips, if you prefer, which usually give a clean cut with minimal crushing. The smaller square sections, though more difficult to drill, also make good fence posts and are less prone to breakages than balsa. They do, however, need to be painted with acrylics or enamels as they tend to repel watercolours.

Matches

These must be among the most popular items ever to be used by the DIY modeller. Even in these scale-orientated days they still have their uses and remain cheap and easy to get hold of. They do seem to vary a bit in size, but the most common brands are usually 38mm long and 2mm square. If they are to be used for fencing that would yield posts of 6in square timber in 9ft 6in lengths, so there is an ample amount that can be buried below the surface. They are rather oversized to form the usual field boundaries with barbed wire, although they do pass muster if they are cut or split in half. Better applications are to use them as the upright supports for wooden fences or, sanded smooth and with a tapered top, drilled to accept 0.2mm plastic rod or florist's wire to represent the typical roadside barriers of concrete and steel pipe.

Some of the other DIY materials that merit a place on the modeller's workbench: fillers, various types of wood (including matchsticks and coffee-stirrers), plasticine and clay.

MODELLING MATERIALS

Plasticine

This is a perfectly straightforward material and large blocks, most commonly in grey or terracotta, may be obtained from art or craft shops for about £2. It tends to fall midway between a material and a tool. In the former role it is useful for cement capping on chimney stacks, into which it is then easy to seat the various pots. Plasticine is simple to sculpt with a palette knife, making it a good choice for creating steps up banks, decorative wall-capping or as an alternative way of scribing stone walls. When making trees I also use it extensively for shaping tree-trunks and main branches around armatures of sedum stems bound together. In its role as a tool it is useful for holding structures upright while the glue sets and for adding weight to wagons, where it also helps to hold other materials in place. Finally, it can make a further contribution to the wagon fleet when used as a base for actual loose loads, such as coal, sand, ballast or stone.

Modelling clay

This is often called 'air-dry clay' since that is what it is designed to do. It may also be bought from art or craft shops, but is usually about twice as expensive as plasticine. Its principal use is as a coating to a card base that can be effectively scribed to represent any chosen form of stonework. This is normally left until the clay is properly dry and hard, usually about twenty-four hours after application. It begins to dry almost as soon as it is exposed to the air, however, and in a warm room, or under a hot tungsten bulb, speed is essential as it quickly becomes unworkable. Seal the bag as soon as you have taken the amount you require or you will have a large rock-hard lump next time you need it.

FILLERS

There are a great many types of fillers available from most DIY outlets and no doubt most modellers will find a use for most of them. The projects described here, however, will require only a ready-mixed lightweight interior filler, which usually comes in either large tubes or resealable tubs. Most major brands produce something of this type, but my preferred version is from Wilco and currently retails at less than £4 for a 600ml tub. It is long lasting and more than adequate for the tasks described in the projects, for example as a scenic surface on background cuttings, roadways and to smooth out the steps where surfaces meet. In diluted form and combined with PVA and paints, it has been used as a surface skim and as a coating for scratch-built walls.

FOAMBOARD

This is an ultra-lightweight substance consisting of a central core of plastic foam laminated between surface layers with a paper-like texture. It is becoming widely available in art or craft shops, usually in white but occasionally in black, as A3 and A1 boards and either singly or in packs. It has nominal thicknesses of 5mm and 10mm, but the latter is hard to find and the former is often closer to 7mm. It is easy to cut with a scalpel or craft knife. Foamboard has many applications, including reinforcing buildings, creating terrain formers and even making complete tabletop baseboards. When using it for baseboards it is best sourced from a local signage company, who will be able to cut it to size from the large sheets supplied by the manufacturer. My portable 'East Ilsley' layout comprises nine scenic boards, each of which measures 4ft 6in x 2ft 6in but weighs barely three or four kilograms even with all the track, buildings and fully detailed landscaping.

PLAY FOAM

This has many different trade names for what is basically the same product. It is soft, child-friendly foam rubber that is very easy to cut and comes as A4 and A3 sheets in a wide variety of colours. The main use that I have found for it is as track underlay, for which it is invariably cheaper and far easier to work than traditional cork. Its thickness of roughly 2mm makes it very convenient for bringing yard surfaces up to sleeper and rail heights. Most art or craft shops stock it and the usual cost is around £1 per sheet.

ASH

If you have access to a coal or wood fire then the finely sieved ash is perfect to represent loco-ash or, mixed with fine ballast, to give the worn-smooth surfaces found in yards and around sheds. If you can't get hold of the real thing, cigarette ash can provide a possible alternative for those who ignore the health warnings.

TINFOIL

Like many other materials, tinfoil comes in a variety of shapes and sizes. Those that are most easily obtained are sold as baking-cases for tarts and muffins, or they can be recycled from supermarket cake and pie dishes. In both types the part we need is the generally flat centre portion, which is cut out and sides are discarded. Roll a round pencil or similar object across the foil until any creases or dents have been smoothed out. The objective is to reproduce the once common sheets of corrugated galvanized iron. The next step is to use the pencil and a ruler to gently scribe as many lines as possible at 1mm intervals on each small workpiece. One always needs quite a lot of finished sheets, so this task is well suited to a batch process. Finally cut out as many rectangles as you can, each measuring roughly 24mm x 12mm to represent the normal sheet size of 6 x 3ft. Save any offcuts as some may still be usable. The finished sheets can be fixed to any wall or roof using smears of any clear glue; they may need to be pressed down to get them all suitably flat, but don't press too hard or you risk spoiling those vital grooves. They can be painted with enamels or acrylics but may require an initial spray of primer. It is worth noting that it is almost impossible to source 4mm scale metal tin: I have only found one packet in the last fifty years.

POLYSTYRENE PLATES

When extracted from its decorative rim, the flat centre portion of the picnic plates sold by supermarkets can be glued to any card template and lightly scribed to give a very passable version of stone walling. It will accept water colours, but these may give better results if applied on top of an emulsion paint primer. This material is very easy to work and is much lighter than card of the same thickness, but it is rather fragile and needs careful handling until it's safely installed on the layout.

Many items can be put to a good use even though it may be far removed from their intended roles, such as polystyrene picnic plates, tinfoil baking cases, cottons and string, nylon thread, foamboard and children's play foam.

NYLON THREAD

This is a sort of 'superfine cotton' and is fairly easy to buy from craft or sewing shops. Over the years there has been much debate about the best method of representing fence-wire. The general consensus is that cotton is too thick and attracts dust; the alternative of fine fishing line is better but can be difficult to keep straight, becomes brittle over time or when fixed with superglues and is, in any case, almost invisible. It is usable, but with care. Nylon thread has none of these problems and can be tied, glued or threaded with equal ease. It generally comes in brown or black and can be painted with thinned enamels as necessary to show signs of newness or of rusting with age.

FLORIST'S WIRE

This is a soft metal wire used in flower arranging. It comes in a variety of thicknesses, usually in 12in lengths. It is normally found in most craft shops but some larger florists may have a limited selection. It can be bought as multi-packs containing several different thicknesses or as separate packs with greater numbers of just one size. The very thinnest sort is only marginally thicker than the nylon and is an acceptable and easy to use alternative for wire fencing when threaded through wooden or plastic posts. Thicker versions can be used for pipework or, as I use it, for hook couplings and vacuum or steam-heating pipes.

The best advice I can give about materials is to be resourceful and try anything that looks promising. This may seem a lot of effort when compared to buying a named product from a model shop, but it is worth remembering that a commercial product may not exactly match your specific requirements. It is far more satisfying to discover your own solution.

FINISHES

This is the area that falls between the two fields of 'materials' on the one hand and 'tools' on the other. It is true that some materials are almost finishes in their own right, but even these need a little bit of extra effort to obtain the best results. The following list includes both DIY and off-the-shelf products, since each will find a role for both the kit-assembler and the scratch-builder.

PAINTS

Primers

These are the brush, spray or aerosol paints that are vital when preparing metal items for final painting with enamels, acrylics or watercolours. In our particular context, however, these are not generally needed since metal does not figure in our projects, apart from tin sheets. For our purposes primers are base coats or undercoats designed to give a better result to the final finish. We need to consider only two possible candidates: the matt white enamel used as the base coat on plastic or metal figures, and any suitable matt emulsion that we can use scenically or, as needed, on structures made from card.

Enamels

These need no explanation and have few applications on these types of projects. Matt white, mentioned above, has a further role in helping to pick out details on ironwork, fencing and telegraph poles. Matt black also has its uses on ironwork and fencing, and in addition helps to create a totally shadowed effect inside buildings. Except for these two essentials, the only other small tins we need are those for the various 'track colours' and the correct house colours for our chosen region or company.

Acrylics

These have now acquired considerable status among the modelling fraternities. They have become viable substitutes for both enamels and watercolours and are widely available in both standard ranges and in specific railway or military ranges. They can be applied by brush or sprayed on, and they give outstanding results in the right hands. If you've not used them before, however, they need a bit of practice and have a tendency to dry quite quickly, clogging up brushes and nozzles. It's sound policy to keep a suitable solvent/cleanser within easy reach.

A wide range of items are available to make life easier for the kit or scratch-builder. These include pre-printed papers, downloads, and a wealth of individual components and accessory packs in plastic, white-metal, brass and, more recently, in laser-cut woods.

Watercolours

These might be considered as more the preserve of artists or children, but, as a long-term modeller, I would hate to be without mine. They vary quite considerably in their quality and characteristics, but this is one case where the most expensive types are not necessarily the best option for our purposes. The two main players are Winsor & Newton and Rowney: both market a huge range of colours in either tubes or their solid equivalent, known as 'pans'. Below these there are numerous opportunities to buy cheaper, but quite acceptable, alternatives from the emerging discount art shops. The main use for watercolour is as the finish for scratch-built card structures, but I also use it on almost all my figures. If you are just starting out and wondering what to buy, I would suggest getting a smallish and inexpensive box or palette with about a dozen colours. This would be adequate, but I would suggest buying an additional small tube of Chinese White, which is always useful to soften and tone down the brighter hues. (Brushes will be discussed below with the other tools.) The other important application for these paints is to colour the exposed white edges that are so much in evidence on card kits. The manufacturers usually suggest treating these with felt-tip pens, but I can't go along with this as they are nearly all in bright primary colours and tend to dry with a slight shine, which makes the end result almost as obvious as the original fault. Watercolours enable you to get an almost exact match and, of course, dry completely matt.

PASTELS

These can be bought singly or in sets and, like water-colours, are variable in both quality and price. It is worth scanning the shelves in stores such as Range or Hobbycraft to find their cheaper sets of neutral tones. These are available in both 'cool' tones (black through descending shades of grey towards white) and 'warm' tones (dark brown through descending rusty hues to cream). Ideally both are useful for all the weathering tasks to which we can assign them, from locos and rolling stock, buildings and scenic settings, right down to subtle shading on figures. If you can't find any suitable sets, then buy them individually in decent range of tones. You should always choose a greyish-blue, which is perfect for sunlit sooty roofs.

PENCILS

These are more tools than finishes but they are useful for weathering engines and rolling stock. The shiny graphite traces they leave behind are ideal for representing the wear on metal from the constant contact with human hands and hobnail boots, for example on steps, ladders, handrails, handles and latches. (The main uses for pencils will be described below.)

TALCUM POWDER

This is a useful weathering aid and can represent dust on vehicles, rolling stock and buildings. To be really effective, however, it is best applied to matt surfaces and some practice is required to get the best results. It is extremely cheap and easy to use since any errors or shortcomings can be quickly wiped off with a damp cloth. It is definitely environmentally friendly and certainly makes your workbench smell nice.

COMMERCIALLY PRODUCED FINISHES

There are more than enough of these to constitute a whole section and the selection is continually growing. They can be divided into two distinct groups, both of which are widely available in model shops or online. The first group includes all the various liquids and powders that can be applied to models in much the same way as the more DIY items already discussed. They are extremely effective and can be purchased as single pots or in small sets of interrelated tones. Their downside is that they are quite expensive and, since a little goes a long way, you may well be spending much more than

Types of paints that can be used range from DIY 'match-pots' to top quality enamels or acrylics in specific colours. Wherever possible you should test them first to ensure you have the right paint for the job.

The most widely used of all the colourants on my own workbench are watercolours and pastels. It isn't necessary to invest in the more expensive products, since in many cases cheaper versions will do the job just as well, if not better. Mine are used for everything from the brickwork on scratch-built buildings to 'dressing' miniature figures. They are also invaluable for all weathering tasks and for tidying the edges on card kits.

you need. The second group is huge, embracing all the products that can provide an almost instant finish to any building or lineside structure. They are aimed at the scratch-builder or anyone wishing to customize a kit-built or ready-to-plant model. The simplest of these are the basic brick-papers, followed by those with self-adhesive backings. More recent products may have a textured finish. Finally there are plastic sheets that offer full relief detail but need painting. All of these have their uses and they deserve their place in the modeller's stock box. The recent and ongoing expansion of items available to download has greatly increased the variety and quality of what is on offer.

ACCESSORY PACKS

Every modeller will find a use for these as they really do add the finishing details that make all the difference to a building. They are available as plastic mouldings, white metal or photo-etched brass, and cover all the obvious items, such as windows, doors, chimneys, soffits, barge-boards, guttering, downpipes and drainpipes, together with such mundane essentials as water butts and dustbins. Since they are so useful, it's a good idea to keep a stock of them ready for future use.

TOOLS

This is a case where pictures really are worth the proverbial 'thousand words'. Everything that we use to transform all the oddments listed above into fully detailed and realistic buildings is a 'tool'. To produce yet another list would be a tedious exercise, so we'll rely on photographs to show everything from albums to adhesives, pins to paintbrushes, scalpels to set squares. From the outset I would stress, especially to newcomers, that toolkits need not be expensive. Almost everything used on the projects, and indeed on my two main layouts, has come from pound-shops, market tool-stalls and other inexpensive specialist outlets. Their quality may sometimes leave something to be desired, but they are cheap to replace and more than adequate for our requirements.

Field research is unbeatable if the structures you want to recreate are still accessible. A typical kit to put in the car might include maps and guides, camera and notepad, tape measure and measuring-stick. If you will be working in a live environment you should also have a high visibility safety vest.

Desk research can take many forms. The most likely starting-point will be general books, photo-albums and magazines, which will give you an initial broad overview and provide the inspiration to extend your searches to the next level.

As you get closer to deciding on your ultimate goal, you will need to concentrate on sources specifically relevant to your project.

The monthly model press is an invaluable way of keeping up with your fellow modellers and hearing about the latest products, tips and techniques. Some of the journals are also linked to online chat rooms and forums.

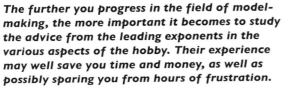

The further you progress in the field of model-making, the more important it becomes to study the advice from the leading exponents in the various aspects of the hobby. Their experience may well save you time and money, as well as possibly sparing you from hours of frustration.

One of the great advantages of modelling with card, whether from kits or scratch-built, is that there is no need for expensive tools or workshop facilities. Almost everything you will ever need, such as these cutting tools, will be found here. None of it is expensive or hard to find, and you could probably find it all on the average high street or on a market stall for less than £10.

Among the various planning and drawing aids available, you will find that Peco point plans are invaluable. Many other useful planning aids may be found by searching online.

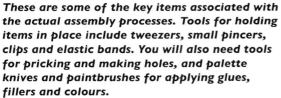

These are some of the key items associated with the actual assembly processes. Tools for holding items in place include tweezers, small pincers, clips and elastic bands. You will also need tools for pricking and making holes, and palette knives and paintbrushes for applying glues, fillers and colours.

Expensive adhesives intended for a particular task are being introduced all the time, but they are not really necessary. John Ahern, for example, built the whole of 'Madder Valley' using only simple Seccotine and that has lasted for seventy years. All you need is PVA, glue sticks, paper glue and a clear or 'universal' glue like UHU. A hot glue gun is the perfect tool if you have many bits to fix in a hurry.

There may be some tasks that are better accomplished with one of the more specialized adhesives. Plastics, for example, may need polystyrene cement, available in tubes or bottles, while metal objects may require a two-part epoxy adhesive. Cyanos/superglues will stick anything, especially careless fingers.

CHAPTER TWO

GOODS WORKINGS IN THE STEAM ERA

SETTING THE SCENE

In the introduction we selected 'railway-like' and 'prototypical' as terms to describe the overall aims of our layouts and their operations. Since this book is chiefly concerned with the recreation of goods workings and their attendant facilities, some broad descriptions of these essential services would not seem out of place. Those of us who frequented the lineside in the 1950s will doubtless have our own memories to call upon. If however, you were born during the present reign, then such experiences will be before your time.

It would have been convenient to direct the modeller to just a few key albums filled with images of these long-vanished trains, but unfortunately the humble goods trains were rarely captured by the photographers of the period – and even more rarely in colour. Despite the fact that freight accounted for at least 60 per cent of traffic, however, there are some very good reasons for this apparent neglect.

Cameras and film were still in short supply and the equipment needed to obtain decent and publishable images was either large and cumbersome or even more scarce. The few photographers who possessed the necessary resources tended, somewhat naturally, to focus their lenses on the more glamorous express locomotives heading main-line passenger trains. There were other factors that contributed to this dearth of

Goods trains like this plodded their way around the whole country. They were limited to maximum speeds of just 25mph for those without any vacuum-braked vehicles and 35mph for those with not less than four 'fitted' next to the engine. Trains such as this were often headed by locomotives near to retirement, such as this elderly ex-GWR 4-4-0. They are easy to replicate in model form on any region.

'Mogul' 2-6-0s were always intended for 'mixed traffic' duties. Some sheds might keep them in good condition for more prestige workings, while others would use them for anything needed, such as this local coal service in Wales. BEN BROOKSBANK; LICENSED FOR REUSE UNDER THIS CREATIVE COMMONS LICENCE

images, especially in the earlier years of our chosen period. Working hours, for example, were much longer than today so the time available to wait beside the line was more restricted. To that must be added the fact that much main-line goods traffic tended to be moved at night. The days were given over to the making-up of trains in the major goods and marshalling yards, leaving the main lines clear to provide speedy passage for public passenger services.

All that aside, there were still some major routes that carried freight on relief or goods lines and on other routes that perhaps had more sparse passenger services. There were also many goods services that enjoyed a greater priority or could simply plod along in the wake of even the slowest 'all stations stopper'. Trains like these have indeed been immortalized on camera and a keen reader or researcher should certainly be able to locate sufficient photos to provide some inspiration, if not to recreate them faithfully, but this type of research will take longer.

The greatest contributor towards that elusive 'railway-like' atmosphere on any layout is surely

the well-modelled goods train. This is especially true when it is worked in the 'prototypical' manner appropriate to its consist. To achieve it is necessary to thumb through every relevant book or magazine, taking brief notes, photocopying the page or leaving a post-it note in place to make it easier to find again.

During our chosen period from roughly the mid-1940s to the onset of the 1960s the railways as a whole were subject to enormous change. Nowhere was this change more pronounced than in the movement of goods and raw materials, in the wagon fleets that conveyed them, and among the locomotive stock needed to haul them. In January 1948 the newly created British Railways inherited more than 1,100,000 goods wagons, ranging from antiques dating back to the mid-nineteenth century to the massive specialist stock designed to carry tanks and naval guns in the two World Wars. This enormous pool was not only made up of entire wagon fleets from the 'Big Four' (GWR, LMS, LNER and SR), but also comprised the tens of thousands of trucks that had previously been classed as 'private owners'. The degree of unwanted or unjustifiable duplication was horrendous. Research has shown that most wagons were standing idle during this period for as long as thirteen days between loads, and even then it might involve only a part-load rather than a full wagon. The cost of this excess capacity would fall squarely on the new British Railways. The end-users themselves cleared their loads as quickly as possible, usually within three days, as they were still subject to demurrage – the railway equivalent of an excess parking charge – if they failed to comply.

A further problem for the BR board was the age and poor condition of much of the stock. The vast majority consisted of patched and repaired, wooden-bodied four-wheel wagons that had quite literally been worked to death during the six years of war. The only answer was to embark on a massive programme of scrapping this duplicated, obsolete and decrepit fleet. This would take many years to complete as the whole lot couldn't be dealt with in one blow. Some would have to be patched-up yet again and left in service until sufficient quantities of more modern stock could emerge as replacements.

POTENTIAL AND CHANGE

While all this undoubtedly gave the railways a headache, it nonetheless provides fertile opportunities for the modeller. Throughout the whole of the earlier part of our period – say 1945 to 1955 – an almost infinite variety of stock was deployed across the nation's goods trains. Dilapidated ex-private owner wagons and equally battered former 'Big Four' company wagons ran buffer-to-buffer with the new replacements emerging from the various BR works and the contractors' factories. In addition to this variety was the simple fact that there was an awful lot of it. Mixed goods trains would rarely be less than sixty wagons long and often eighty or more would be the norm. Even the more prestigious fast traffic would run to more than forty four-wheelers. Yet more evidence of the vastness of this fleet can be seen in images of goods and marshalling yards full to the brim with stock.

The keen modeller, like all enthusiastic shoppers in these acquisitive days, can easily justify the purchase of as much goods stock as can be squeezed

Bulleid's revolutionary Pacifics were another engine type very loosely described as 'mixed traffic', but they were rarely used on anything other than express freights and milk workings. This one is on humble duties on a special-goods train on the preserved Swanage Railway.

The bogie brake-vans of the old Southern Railway were affectionately known as 'Queen Marys', or just plain 'Marys', after their apparent similarity to the famous ocean-liner of the time. They remained in service well beyond the end of steam, finding work with the Engineer's Department. This one is always assigned to the ex-Fawley oil trains on the author's 'Wessex Lines'.

on the layout or stored within easy reach. The only restrictive caveats concern buying the right kind of wagons in their appropriate ratios, having the budgets to afford them and then having the time and patience to weather and generally 'distress' them into their more prototypical states. Straight-from-the-box wagons simply won't do, unfortunately, unless you want your 1950s trains to look like the shiny photo-specials glimpsed on the tourist lines of our present century.

Throughout this period the transformation of the real railway became ever more obvious. Of course nothing happened overnight, but it is generally reckoned that 1955 was a watershed in the fortunes of rail freight. Up until then the loss of traffic to the roads, coupled with the slow decline in some industries, was having its effect, but that average annual loss (about 5 per cent) was hardly noticeable on the lineside. However, the disastrous rail strike of that year produced an almost immediate trade down-

turn, followed by even more cancelled contracts as their renewal dates became due. Then came the Clean Air Act 1956, which restricted the use of the more polluting forms of coal. The further loss of easy export markets to the Commonwealth limited demand. Finally, of course, there was the appointment of Dr Beeching.

Traffic levels began to reduce significantly, leading to the complete cancellation of many regular goods services and the amalgamation of others. Trains became shorter. While wagon-load traffic was discouraged, they were still quite varied in their consists and now almost entirely comprised modern BR types. Many local goods yards began to run out of traffic and even major depots and marshalling yards saw much less activity. Visually, too, the appearance of the trains began to change for the worse. From the locomotives right back to the brake vans, rust and dust was the increasingly common livery of the period.

Without wishing for one moment to discourage any modeller who wants to recreate the goods traffic of the 1960s, for most of us the mid-1950s are quite modern enough. But the sixties enthusiast – diesels and all – can still model the yards and sheds and the vestiges of their former traffic. There is also the opportunity to use the larger express steam locos on freight as they eked out their days before heading to the scrapyard. However, to stay within our remits of 'railway-like' and 'prototypical', those Castles, Duchesses, A4s or Bulleids should run bereft of name plates and, as my grandson would say, 'well mucky'.

UNAVOIDABLE CONSTRAINTS AND KEEPING IT FEASIBLE

Having devoted some space to the general background of goods workings at the time, what of the trains themselves and our ability to recreate them in miniature? It is first necessary to acknowledge that most modellers, if not all, must accept a significant degree of compromise. For all but the privileged few, with space to spare and equally expansive budgets, realistic train lengths are simply not an option. To try to replicate a sixty-wagon 'through freight' might

In the early 1950s Britain's armed forces were still at wartime levels and maintained worldwide commitments. National Service helped maintain the numbers and troop trains were a regular source of railway traffic. This load of Fireflys and Cromwells are en route from Warcop in Cumbria to the ranges at Lulworth on the Dorset coast. The WD is heading a train that is nearly 9ft long.

Heavy and awkward consignments like these required special loading facilities at each end of their journey. They also needed to be secured firmly despite the relatively slow speeds at which they travelled.

easily set one back in excess of £800 from loco to brake van. Moreover, even if you have saved up and or are prepared to set it against a credit card, that little lot will occupy more than 15ft of main line or sidings, rather more than a typical twelve-coach express.

Then we come to the haulage abilities of contemporary ready-to-run (r-t-r) locomotives. Or rather we don't, since even the strongest eight-coupled goods loco currently available would struggle with half that load. Indeed it will cope with barely a quarter of that if the wagons are running with extra scale weight.

For what it is worth, I consider that both my layouts are on the large side of those typically modelled. Nonetheless, despite having a scale length of

one-and-a-half miles at my disposal, the effect of 2ft radius curves, reverse curves, complex point work and the odd gradient impose severe limits on what can be operated realistically and reliably. Experience, perhaps more honestly referred to as 'trial and error', proved pretty conclusively that the average 'long goods' should be around seventeen or eighteen four-wheel wagons plus a brake van, and certainly not more than twenty. That still gives a train length of around 6ft, which means that on the curves through Winterbourne Station the loco and brake-van are going in opposite directions. The extra drag effect, especially with weighted stock that already totals close to 2kg, taxes even my heaviest and most powerful engines.

For this book, at least, I will advise that 'seven-teen-ish' is the workable norm for goods trains. As stated earlier, that doesn't mean that the enthusiastic shopper can't buy lots more lovely new wagons, only that they need to be made up into lots more lovely trains.

This brings us to choosing the trains that could be featured on any 1950s layout together with an indication of the type of loco that might head them. Power for power, most r-t-r locomotives use similar mechanisms and perform to much the same standards, so the various suggestions that are given are simply an attempt to capture the appearance and 'atmosphere' of the working rather than providing a positive recommendation to purchase on grounds of capability.

GETTING IT RIGHT

TRAIN IDENTIFICATION

Almost from the beginning trains running on railways in the United Kingdom were required to carry a clear identification of their type at the front. This had to be visible by both day and night. The best, but not the only, method of achieving this was found to be removable and interchangeable oil lamps. Over the decades this became common practice, together with an almost equal acceptance of a common code. Locomotives built by or for most of the independent railways had three lamp brackets on their front and rear buffer beams, and one on top of the smokebox

Always remember that loose-coupled and part-fitted freights must be tailed by a brake van showing three red lamps to the rear.

immediately ahead of the chimney or at the top of the tender or bunker. The general rule for the codes, certainly by the latter days of the Big Four, involved nothing more complex than placing either a single lamp or two lamps in various patterns on these four available front brackets, or on the rear brackets if running tender/bunker first.

Of course there were exceptions. Some of the more modern engines, for example, could represent the same codes by electric lights. The Southern Railway favoured a more complex system using large white discs or electric lights, often up to three at a time. These were arranged on five brackets, the two additional points being either side of the smokebox. That system not only identified the train types but also indicated the routes they were following. The Somerset and Dorset Railway retained the oil lamps but, not surprisingly, it had its own unique version of the codes.

At the rear of passenger trains, or locomotives running light engine, there would be one single red lamp mounted above the buffers (usually the left or inner one). Its position was not statutory but simply depended upon the bracket most convenient at the departure station. Guards brake vans at the rear of all goods workings carried three lamps: one in a centre bracket showed just red and two higher up on either side showed red to the rear and white to the front. This latter feature enabled the locomotive crew to check that their train was intact. The outer lamp was removed when the train was running on a relief, a goods line or loop-line.

In cases where only one lamp was shown at the front of a locomotive, the spare would be on a bracket on the framing or stowed in the cab. Many locos, including models, have two such spare brackets on the frame. This goes back to the period when the red lamp to be placed at the rear of a light engine movement was a separate item, hence three lamps would be needed: two white, one red. During the 1930s an inventive individual, perhaps working at the GWR shed at Didcot, hit on the idea of simply inserting a red shade on the spare lamp, with an obvious saving of costs and hassle. Incidentally, should you feature a train carrying a member of the Royal Family, all four lamps must be shown at the front.

These basic head codes were unchanged through most of the twentieth century, even into the diesel era. The exact description of the trains represented, however, did see some changes, particularly in the latter years when vacuum-braked stock ('fitted' or 'piped") became more common.

TRAIN TYPES OR 'CLASSES'

It is worth noting here that the visual appearance of many different workings or classes could appear very similar if not almost identical. Mixed goods trains, to give them their familiar but imprecise definition, could be completely loose-coupled, part-fitted with just four piped vehicles next to the engine, or with at least one-third of their vehicles piped. Even though they carried the different class headlamp codes, all three trains may well have had a nearly identical composition and numbers of vans or opens next to the engine. The only real difference would be the vital presence, or otherwise, of the connected vacuum brake. On the layout, of course, such niceties are unimportant since even the most pedantic modeller cannot actually connect up the replica brake pipes. The sole difference is the relative speeds at which they should be run.

The era we are looking at spans the transition between the Big Four and British Railways. This poses quite a few problems when it comes to defining the various lamp codes and their respective classes and descriptions. The old GWR, as it often did, had its own definitions for the classes and the types of workings that they covered. Some of these matched the new BR style, but others did not. I have tried to follow the official BR version that was in force at the time and also included the GWR classes where these coincided. When studying period photographs, however, you will quickly see that the appearance of many workings will look the same even though their lamp codes may be different. Unfortunately the reverse is equally true, with a variety of trains all running under the same lamps. If in doubt, you should replicate what you can discern from your reference images. The details that follow also include some indication of the engine types likely to be in charge of each class.

Class A

Class A headlamps, one over each front buffer, were only carried by workings outside the scope of this book, the most common of which were express passenger trains. Other instances could include: breakdown trains going to clear the line; light engine(s) going to assist a disabled train; empty coaching stock (ECS) cleared to run at express speed; and the nightly express 'newspaper trains', which may perhaps squeeze into our terms of reference,.

Motive power: Any express passenger type from the pre-grouping survivors up to the latest Britannia. For 'holiday extras' and 'second portions' anything might be rostered, including heavy freight locos and even larger tank engines.

Class B

One lamp at the chimney or top of the smokebox. This can, among other things, cover the 'mixed train' sometimes found on branch lines when the normal one or two coaches are tailed by a few goods vehicles. More usually it would cover all the branch passenger or goods trains and the main-line 'stoppers'.

Motive power: On branch lines this would normally be restricted to smaller tank engines and the lighter (often ancient) 0-6-0 tender locos. Main-line stoppers would have engines suitable for the train length, which might be anything from a large tank to a 'namer'. They are often used as 'running in turns', so a King on a 'B' set is acceptable.

Class C

Lamps to chimney and left hand buffer. (Note that in some cases milk trains are also seen running fast under 'D' lamps.) These are the true express freights with every vehicle connected by vacuum brake to the engine or, on certain types of load, with at least one-third of the vehicles piped to the engine. In the first example this would include such workings as parcels, fish, meat, fruit, milk, horseboxes, cattle or perishables. These were usually referred to in railway parlance as 'fully-fitted' trains. The second group, rather obviously called 'part-fitted', could include mixed freight, livestock, perishables and ballast trains. These could easily be identified since they would always have a brake van at the rear, while the fully fitted would more usually run with the obligatory red

The railways carried nearly all the nation's bulk milk supplies, with daily express workings from the countryside to the capital and major cities. A Hall is here seen heading the 'up' Plymouth–Kensington working. At the author's boyhood station, Challow, it was a magnificent sight as the Whitland milk, often with a Castle at the head, hurtled through.

The supply of coal to the cities generated an enormous amount of traffic. No sooner had the coal trains delivered their 'up' loads of 500 or 600 tons than another lengthy rake of empties was on its way back 'down' to the collieries. This working has one of the Western's ubiquitous Moguls at its head. GREAT WESTERN TRUST

tail lamp placed on the last vehicle, as on passenger trains. Both these services were permitted to run at 45mph, but a fully fitted train, with all vehicles of longer wheelbase carrying the 'XP' rating or marks, could run at express speeds of usually about 60mph. **Motive power:** The choice here is very wide and can include any of the express passenger engines, the larger mixed traffic engines and, towards the end of the period, the magnificent BR 9Fs.

Class D

Lamps on the left hand and centre of the buffer beam. These workings covered a whole multitude of freight workings and were a lesser class of 'part-fitted', needing a minimum of just four vacuum-fitted vehicles connected to the engine. They were limited to a maximum speed of 35mph and were always tailed by a brake van.

Motive power: depending upon the load it could be a medium to large mixed traffic tender or even tank engine. Suitably equipped freight locos would also be in evidence.

Class E

Lamps to chimney and right-hand buffer beam. This is almost a 'catch-all' class since it embraces express freight, fish, meat, fruit and cattle, so long as 'class I traffic', such as coal, is included, and provided it isn't running under the C or D codes. It could also include a breakdown crane not going to an accident.

Motive power: This could be anything that was available and able to handle the particular load over the required distance. Avoid rostering the smaller tank engines.

Class F

Lamps to chimney and centre buffer beam. These were a very common sight and are defined as a through fast freight not running under any of the previous codes and carrying a through load to its destination.

A Southern H15 is here seen heading ballast wagons, probably to or from the main quarries at Meldon. This was one of the many varieties of trains that could be seen running under the common 'through fast freight' lamp code. Note how the code is shown by discs rather than lamps, which was quite common when running on other regions' lines. *AUSTIN ATTEWELL*

Another mixed goods, this time behind a Western Region Hall, looks very different. Their almost infinite variety of wagons made them fascinating to watch and a perfect subject for the modeller. *BEN BROOKSBANK; LICENSED FOR REUSE UNDER THIS CREATIVE COMMONS LICENCE*

The 28xx class were among the first and most successful long-distance, heavy-goods engines to operate on the nation's railways. One of their major tasks was to haul the 100-wagon (1000 ton) coal trains from South Wales to London.
GREAT WESTERN TRUST

One of the rarely seen Western 47xx class 'Night Owls' works back to London with a rake of wagons that seem to disappear into the distance. It's worth observing the preponderance of sheeted-opens in the consist and again those same through-lights. *GREAT WESTERN TRUST*

Motive power: This code was commonly seen on lengthy coal or mineral workings and their returning 'empties', often headed by the big 2-8-0s, WDs and BR 9Fs.

Class G

One lamp in the centre of the buffer beam. This might be seen on a light engine or engines, or an engine and brake van. In certain areas it also covered the 'workmen's train'.

Motive power: Any loco or locos(s) making the trip as a light engine, from a pannier to a Pacific.

'Tripping' spare brake vans would most likely be headed by a yard pilot (a small tank engine) or a freight loco en route to the yard.

Class H

Lamps to centre and right of buffer beam. This was another frequently seen code covering any freight, minerals, ballast or 'empties' taken as a through load to its destination.

Motive power: Any goods or mixed traffic engine that was available.

This 28xx on the troughs near Goring, in Oxfordshire, is carrying yet another 'fast freight' head code. These codes can be a nightmare for the keen modeller who is trying to get things right. The best advice is always to work from a photograph since then you know that it happened at least once. On my own 'Wessex Lines' it may seem that I am fooling visitors by putting a grimy WD on the down 'Cornish Riviera', but it did once happen when a King failed at Taunton and it was the only spare engine.
GREAT WESTERN TRUST

Modellers wanting one of these long-lived Southern 'Black Motors' or '700s' have had to make do with an ancient white-metal kit, but a ready-to-run version is imminent. This '700' may have only just collected its train since it seems to be carrying the Class 'G' light-engine single lamp – or perhaps the fireman forgot to place the other one.
AUSTIN ATTEWELL

Very different trains could operate under the same lamps. The Class 'K' working covers all ordinary freights as long as they are expecting to stop at intermediate stations. The pick-up goods is a typical example and this pannier tank has clearly earned a drink with such a heavy train. AUSTIN ATTEWELL

In complete contrast to the pannier in the previous picture, this little 14xx is happily trundling along with a trip freight weighing little more than itself. If your budget runs to only a very small layout, this is the prototype working for you. GREAT WESTERN TRUST

Class J

Lamp to left of the buffer beam. Used for through freight, mineral or ballast stopping at intermediate stations. In some cases this could be described as the 'pick-up goods' or 'fly'. The old GWR, however, used this code to cover the regular morning and evening 'workmen's trains'. Note also the subtle variation between this and the next code, which depends upon the distinction and definition of 'intermediate stations' or 'local stations'. This will probably be of little concern to any modeller with the usual one-station layout.

Motive power: If the run was a reasonably short distance this would usually be one of the tank engines. Tender locos did appear, but were not popular if much shunting was involved.

Class K

One lamp to the right of the buffer beam. Used for ordinary freight, mineral or ballast trains stopping at local stations, for branch goods trains or for pilot trips. It was mandatory for all engines moving around the shed or motive power depot, or en route from there to pick up its train.

Motive power: This will depend entirely on the type of activity being carried out.

The accompanying diagram shows how these lamp codes might appear on your own trains. It is more than likely that you will be using the appropriate lamps from the Springside range. These, however, have very over-sized handles and are much too clean. Try to carefully pick away the excess paint and file the handles to a finer profile. To complete the effect, give the lamp a quick wash with some dirty thinners.

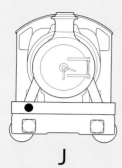

J

Through freight, mineral or ballast, stopping at intermediate stations.

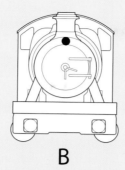

B

Mixed train, or breakdown (**not** going to clear line).

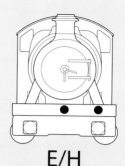

E/H

Freight, mineral, ballast, or empties carrying through load to destination.

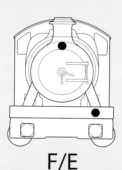

F/E

Express freight, fish, meat, fruit or cattle (or ballast), not running under 'C' or 'D' lamps.

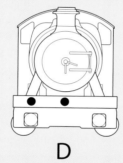

D

Express freight or ballast– (semi or part fitted) with not less than 4 vehicles.

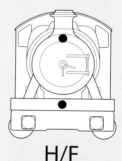

H/F

Through fast freight not running under 'C', 'D' or 'E' codes.

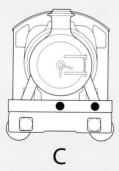

C

Parcels, fish, meat, fruit, milk, livestock, perishables fully fitted

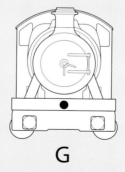

G

Light engine(s) or engine and brake-van(s).

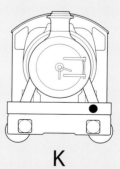

K

Ordinary freight, mineral or ballast stopping at local stations (pick-up goods 'fly'). Branch freight or Pilot trip.

There are many interpretations of the lamp codes displayed during our chosen era and much information is available for those who wish to be more precise in terms of time and place.

MODELLING THE COMPLETE GOODS TRAIN

Having looked briefly at goods workings as a whole and identified the way in which they were classified and described in the steam railway era, it is now time to see how we might realistically replicate them. If your model is only a simple single-line branch, almost every goods train could run under class J or K lights, depending on your period. At a pinch a class B mixed train could make an appearance and, if there happened to be docks or a significant industrial user at the end, then one might be able to justify one of the more main-line codes for an inbound or outbound special or 'through traffic to destination'.

It doesn't really matter if your layout has a fiddle or storage yard, or whether your trains stay in boxes to be assembled on the layout as required. What does matter is that they have the appropriate consist, look 'right', are correctly lamped and have a brake van attached where necessary. The one thing that will be impossible in almost every instance is to replicate the length. As mentioned above, very few layouts, even at club level, can run lengthy sixty- to eighty-wagon goods rakes. Those that might stretch to such extreme lengths would than doubtless struggle to find a locomotive that could pull them.

Each modeller will need to find their own optimum length of trains based on a compromise between layout size, realistic appearance, amount of stock, storage space and, of course, the availability of suitable locomotives to haul them. I can only speak from my experience, but over the years I have found that sixteen to twenty four-wheelers best suits my own layout. Even that modest length occupies around 6ft and, with weighted loaded stock, puts 1.5 to 2kg on the drawbar. Of course some workings, particularly some 'specials' or the 'pick-up', are more lightly loaded, while full coal and its reciprocal empties have consists to the limits of visual realism and haulage capabilities.

It is almost impossible to recommend exactly how many goods wagons the average modeller should aspire to own. It is equally impossible to say how many of each type should be included within the total. We have just suggested that the optimum length of our goods trains will be an important element. However, there is another factor that should always be paramount when considering another purchase: the back story to the layout. You should decide where the layout, whether hypothetical or otherwise, is supposed to be located. What sort of industries and communities does it connect and serve? What lies beyond that little slice of England, or Scotland, or Wales, and how might it generate particular traffic to flow along the lines? If, for example, it is located somewhere between a coalfield and an industrial city, then the frequency of full and empty workings of coal trains will be proportionally high. In the same vein, it is less likely that we would see express milk, fish or the much loved clay trains.

CHOOSING THE STOCK

There are a few guidelines that might help here. Open wagons, whether the old wooden-bodied or the newer metal-bodied types, will outnumber all others by a significant amount (as much as five to one) against the general purpose vans, both fitted or otherwise, which come next. Specialist vehicles, such as fruit or ventilated vans, horseboxes, cattle trucks, milk or oil tanks, bolsters, flats and 'wells', will be few and far between. It is regrettable that the r-t-r manufacturers continuously offer these appealing specials but fail to reflect the sheer volumes of more mundane types that were the mainstay of the real railway.

Despite this shortfall, however, we should acknowledge that we can run our railway in any way we wish as long as it looks right. Rather than specify individual models from particular manufacturers, the following examples are intended to show what can be done to create realistic and railway-like trains that could appear under each of the various classes and descriptions.

Milk

In this period these would be made up of the typical six-wheel glass-lined tanks. Each region had its own particular designs, but the majority of r-t-r examples appear to be closest to those of the GWR. The

This is the first of a series of images of the author's layout intended to reproduce the steam-era photographs shown above. County of Middlesex is the regular motive power on my version of the 'milk'. The tanks are all weathered and weighted: the nineteen six-wheelers and Hawksworth passenger brake add up to nearly 2kg behind the tender.

railways owned the running-gear but the tanks were owned by the actual milk-producing companies and this is reflected in the private owner liveries currently available. Trains were made up of individual or small numbers of tanks off the branches, combining at a suitable station or marshalling yard into the through working to the capital. Typical loads would be no more than sixteen or seventeen tanks since, when full, they have a weight of nearly 30 tons, similar to that of a carriage, plus a passenger full-brake. Use was also made of road-rail tanks, which were trailer-tanks initially hauled by road and then winched on to a modified six-wheel chassis. Churn traffic was certainly still plentiful into the early 1950s and offers very different looking trains to the modeller. These could include six-wheel siphons, insulated vans and bogie-siphons. In both cases these would run under the same class C code and the tail lamp would be fixed to the last vehicle. Returning empties held the same priority and all workings would invariably have a 6P or 7P top-link passenger locomotive at the head. Incidentally, most milk trains were pretty filthy and any corporate or company liveries were often almost completely obscured. The gleaming white tanks so often seen on layouts are far removed from reality.

Meat

The meat trains were a familiar site on any trunk route connecting docks to a major city: London's Smithfield Market was an obvious destination. Britain was importing meat from all over the world, both from the Commonwealth, including Canada, Australia and New Zealand, and from foreign countries, especially Argentina. These workings, like some other examples to follow, were the origins of the post-Beeching 'block trains'. The stock usually

I could not resist the challenge of kit-bashing this lovely little brake, spotted online during a browsing sessions, from a Ratio GWR four-wheel coach.

The 'Kensington Brake' now runs as part of the 'local milk' catering for the still quite heavy churn traffic and also the odd tank from the smaller dairies. The elderly Earl class seen here, named Comet after the one allocated to Didcot, is a fine example of the bargains that may be found at toy fairs. It had been part completed, with the motor and gears put in backwards, and as an abandoned project cost just £10.

remained intact and consisted of refrigerated vans usually classified as 'XP' and capable of running to express schedules. All the old companies and BR had their own designs for vans, but perhaps the ex-GWR 'Micas' are the most familiar. Originally, and not surprisingly, the basic livery was 'white' to indicate refrigerated traffic, but, as with milk tanks, the vans should be well weathered from their frequent use. In some cases meat would also be contained in insulated containers carried on special four-wheel flat trucks. Motive power would again be provided by the express link of 6P or 7P locomotives: it was a common sight to see more than twenty vans behind the tender.

Fish

This is another case of trains running specifically from their respective fishing ports to the city markets. In the days of the Big Four the ventilated vans, usually but not always long-wheelbase four-wheelers, would be painted in coach liveries and were also rated 'XP', since fish traffic demanded a speedy journey. When they had just raced through a wayside station at 60mph there was never any doubt about their load. Where available, the originating shed would roster a locomotive from the express link or at least a mixed traffic engine in good condition.

Fruit

In the steam era the UK still boasted an extensive and well-dispersed fruit industry. Unlike today's globally supported supermarket produce, this traffic would be very seasonal. Nonetheless, most trunk lines would see their fair share of complete fruit trains at some time of the year. The loads would be conveyed either in specially designed 'fruit vans' or in more general-purpose ventilated vans. Some produce might also be conveyed in 'XP' rated bogie passenger full brakes or their four-wheel or six-wheel counterparts.

Motive power should again come from the top end of the stock list. Such was the almost unpredictable seasonality of the crops, however, and hence the sudden demand for trains, that sheds were often pressured into supplying their best available at the time, or borrowing a better foreign engine that had come in off another working.

At the time there was a demand for regular express trains of refrigerated vans to carry imported meat from the Commonwealth and South America. As with the milk trains, they were dispatched as soon as they were ready, so they were commonly seen during the day. These elderly Hornby Dublo MICAs have a 93xx Mogul at the front, but a Hall or even a Castle would have been more usual.

Two special fruit trains deserve a mention. Bananas were bought by the boatload from the West Indies to Bristol or Liverpool and then conveyed in special steam-heated vans to continue the ripening en route. These vans were often owned by Fyffes, the main shippers, but in all cases they carried the distinctive white disc indicating steam-heated and were rated 'XP'. They required a 'big engine'. In complete contrast, anyone who is modelling somewhere in south-west England might like to include the seasonal 'broccoli specials'. These were the traffic department's nightmare. Almost every branch and wayside goods yard became a railhead, and the demand for vans was so great that often complete trains would comprise washed and cleaned cattle trucks. Motive power coming up from the west could be anything from a work-stained, wheezing Mogul to one of the mighty 47xx 2-8-0 'Night Owls'.

Livestock

Complete livestock trains were somewhat of a rarity, since there was little demand for transporting several hundred animals together to the same destination. Nonetheless, it was an important source of traffic. Cattle and sheep, and even pigs and non-thoroughbred horses, would be conveyed in the once familiar cattle trucks. They would usually be destined for a major livestock market or taken from there to the slaughterhouse. One feature worth mentioning is that these trains, if running over long distances, had to make regular stops to water and possibly feed the animals.

Racing thoroughbreds had their own special vehicles, usually conveying two precious animals together with an attendant groom or travelling lad in his own compartment. Horsebox traffic was always in the appropriate XP or full passenger livery and was usually well maintained. Some trainers even had their own specially branded boxes on permanent hire. While most race traffic was conveyed as head- or tail-loads attached to suitably scheduled passenger trains, complete horsebox workings were not unknown. These would be relatively short trips from a junction or busy station out to a major two- or three-day race meeting at an adjacent course. Such prestige workings (perhaps in case the chairman's horse was running) might

well attract an immaculate top-link loco ahead of its duties on the actual race-day 'specials'.

Vans and 'perishables'

These could comprise an enormous range of products and produce. These would be loaded in vans (or in some cases even in sheeted-opens) and could be anything from a full vanload of cheese or potatoes to large bogie siphons filled with flowers, flour, cakes and biscuits, or crates of beer. It could be any combination of loads in quantities that did not justify a complete train. They would usually be part fitted and so limited to 45mph rather than the express speeds of the 'XP' fully fitted workings. They would be more likely to have a mixed-traffic loco at the front and a brake van at the rear. It would not be unusual for a forty- or fifty-vehicle train to have no two vans of the same type together. Vans of all styles and weights from each of the Big Four could be seen on these trains all over the country. These workings often covered very large distances; the daily Penzance–Crewe was a typical example.

Parcels

We hear a great deal about the large volumes of parcels generated for Royal Mail and all the other road carriers, being down to internet shopping. Despite its scale, I doubt if it compares with the vast amount of rail-borne parcels carried in the 1950s. In the weeks leading up to Christmas the stations and depots in most cities and large towns overflowed with parcels from the GPO (Royal Mail) and private firms. Complete trains made up of four-wheel, six-wheel, bogie vans and passenger full brakes would be dispatched throughout the night, often at hourly intervals. As the peak period built up, these would also be slotted in, using XP-rated stock, with the main-line passenger services and were a regular feature even during daylight hours. The normal motive power could be anything from a 'Black Five' to a Duchess or B1 to an A4 'Streak'.

Mixed goods ('fasts')

These could well be those fast freights running with just a few vacuum-fitted vehicles (a minimum of four) next to the engine. In railway terms this

Complete trains of cattle wagons were rarely seen except close to a major market or slaughterhouse. Nonetheless, they provide plenty of visual interest and several different types of stock are always available in kit form. Don't forget that if you have 'loaded' cattle wagons in your working it must be stopped at regular intervals to feed and water the stock.

was a 'fitted head' and the remaining train could be made up of almost anything required within the working. It is more than justifiable to include other vacuum-braked vehicles within the consist, although their pipes would not be connected. Any mix of vans, sheeted-opens, opens and specialist stock can be sorted behind whatever mixed traffic locomotive is to hand. Indeed, even pure freight locos could be seen, since classes such as the ex-LMS 8F or even the ancient Churchward 28xxs of the Western could easily manage the 35mph maximum assigned to the class D trains. Remember these must carry the proper three-lamped brake van, or two lamps if you are lucky enough to have goods or relief lines on your layout.

Mixed goods, coal, empties and block workings

These could be seen running under almost all of the many freight lamp codes. They can comprise another group of freights with 'through loads to destination'. These cover the whole multitude of mixed goods, minerals, ballast trains and empties that plodded up and down the railways every day of the year. Even the most exhaustive survey of

the available steam-era albums, books and magazines would probably fail to identify any common composition for these various workings. Following my own interpretation of the rule book, I limit my class E trains to china clay, ballast and bulk oil alone. In respect of the latter, always include barrier wagons – perhaps two empty opens – next to the engine. You can also add two more at the rear, since these were often block trains and would work back empty in the same formation with the loco and brake van swopping ends.

The class F lamps certainly seem to feature on many if not all of the loaded coal trains and even the returning empties. They can also be found adorning the front of mixed goods workings. These are loose-coupled rakes and are limited to just 25mph. On the trunk routes they would be confined, wherever possible, to plodding along the relief lines. If no relief line existed, then they could be run onto a loop line or backed into a refuge siding to allow faster freights and passenger trains to overtake.

Ordinary freight and pick-up goods

This single-lamped class of train can be justified in any model setting. The official definition is for an 'ordi-

Horseboxes were invariably rated as 'XP' and could therefore be attached to convenient passenger trains. Large race meetings might see these boxes assembled into special workings as they neared their destinations. As can be seen from the lamp code, my little MSWJ engine has clearly come off the branch to take these Hornby, Lima and Wrenn examples down the main line.

nary' freight, which can easily include branch goods trains, local coal or other minerals and the routine 'Sunday working' ballast trains. It can also indicate the banker or pilot engine trips to assist another engine. In every case except the last, where the loco needs a tail lamp, the brake van is about the only regular component: you can put whatever you like behind the tender. Just invent a suitable consist that properly reflects your overall back story. Remember too that these trains call at 'intermediate stations', hence it is the correct code for your pick-up goods or fly. An up-train would almost certainly include a few coal wagons for domestic or commercial users, the odd van or two, maybe a cattle wagon, perhaps some timber or a 'Lowmac' with a new tractor or military vehicle. The choice of motive power is equally wide and could justify a larger goods loco on a train that had no need to actually stop at your wayside station, except to let something faster go past. Generally though, the pick-up goods would favour a small to medium tank engine that is more suited to shunting.

Class G and light engines

Our final classification can cover whatever is appropriate to your back story. Light engine (or engines coupled together) movements were

not exactly popular movement since they occupied track without earning any revenue. But they did happen and they provide a good excuse to parade otherwise idle locos. On a continuous run layout such a working can add a touch of realism to what was otherwise a simple bit of testing a loco or section of track. For variety you can also put a brake van (or vans) on the back – correctly lamped, of course. The movements can be tender or bunker first, in which case the front lamp goes on the back and the obligatory red moves up to the front buffer.

Regional identity

This is only a personal interpretation of the almost infinite variety of composition (consists) that can run within the respective class or headlamp code. Since my own layouts are largely Great Western Railway or British Railways (Western Region), the locos selected inevitably reflect this. The range of models available as r-t-r in today's market, however, offer the appropriate engines no matter what region or company you happen to favour. Regional identities are also revealed at the other end of the trains in the style of the brake vans. Nothing screams 'GWR' more loudly than their ubiquitous

Van traffic is an easy subject and interesting to model. It was quite common to see lengthy trains in which no two vehicles appeared the same. Since loaded vans travelled the length and breadth of the country, typical Southern Railway types could easily turn up in Aberdeen. Trains of returning empty stock might well include specialist vehicles like meat, fish or steam-banana in their consists.

and uniquely styled brake vans, universally known as 'Toads' (their old telegraphic code name). Equally only the Southern Railway had the big 25-ton bogie brake vans known as 'Queen Marys' or, simply, 'Queens'. In general these vans tended to stay within their own territories, often being marked as 'Not Common User' and branded for their home territories. You would be hard put to justify a Plymouth-labelled 'Toad' trundling along behind a coal train in Yorkshire.

USING YOUR RESEARCH

Earlier we discussed the merits of research as a vital aid to getting our goods trains, short though they may be, working as much like the prototype as possible. When composing my own trains for 'Wessex Lines' and, later, for 'East Ilsley' I found it useful to develop a sort of shorthand to describe the trains I had chosen from the various albums, magazines or even archive DVDs. Being blessed with a half-century

Remember that vans were often built as loose-coupled or vacuum-braked versions of the same basic design. The slower classes of van traffic (part-fitted or unfitted) would often be seen behind ordinary goods engines rather than a mixed-traffic type.

Many workings conveyed van traffic from one region to another. These provide an excellent opportunity to feature the locomotives of different companies on your layout. This 8F has brought its vans down from somewhere in the Midlands. Its Western-influenced design is underlined by the fact that it represents one of the wartime builds turned out by Swindon.

of accumulated rolling stock, I was able to make up the various trains as permanent rakes. Since I was lacking a fiddle yard, however, each train was allocated its own drawer in my stock of A4-sized office stationery boxes. Each drawer was then labelled with its description/working, class, the actual stock, the total weight/length and presence, or otherwise, of the brake van.

In case you are tempted to take a similar approach to the one I adopted, my coding system was 'alpha-based', but I'm sure a numeric system would probably work just as well.

Sometimes, if I was feeling really keen, I would also add a prefix 'L' for low-sided or 'H' for high-sided.

When using this system to summarize the train I would include the loco type, class of train and, if possible, the number of vehicles. Using an appropri-

ate photo, a typical entry would look like this, with the loco identified by type or by its actual number:

3030(K) 36 – 3 O(c); 2 V; 1 V(v); 2 O(e); 3 St(c); 2 f(c); 4 V; 2 Cat; 2 Tnk; 3 O(c); 2 O(s); 2 V; 1 O(s); 4 St(c); 2 V; Bv

When assembling this working from the stock box it was necessary to halve the number of vehicles to make up my optimum 'seventeen-ish', including the brake. The choice was quite arbitrary, but I wanted to capture the essential hotchpotch of stock. This was the result, also showing the 'scale tons':

3030(K) 17 – 3 O(c); 2 V; 1 O(e); 2 f(c); 2 V; 1 Cat; 2 Tnk; 2 O(s); 1 V; BV wt incl Bv 1215g (240+ tons) length 65in

Wagon Type	Load	Code
Wooden opens	empty	O(e)
	coal	O(c)
	coal empty	O(ce)
	sheeted	O(s)
	scrap	O(sc)
	timber	O(t)
	clay	O(cl)
	clay empties	O(cle)
Steel opens	as above, but with SO prefix	SO(e) etc
Vans	ordinary	V
	vacuum-fitted	V(v)
	fruit	V(f)
Siphons, etc.		Siph (F, C, H etc)
Carriage truck		CCT
Car carrying		Mogo
Special wagons	flat empty	f(e)
	flat container	f(c)
	flat vehicle(s) etc	f(load described)
	bogie bolster empty	bb(e)
	bogie bolster timber	bb(t)
	bogie bolster steel	bb(st)
	well-wagon empty	ww(e)
	well-wagon loaded	ww(load described)
	crocodile empty	cr(e)
	crocodile loaded	cr(load described)
	oil tank	tnk
	milk tank	mk
	cattle truck	cat
	horseboxes	hb
	brake vans	bv

While none of this is in any way an essential exercise for a railway modeller, it is nonetheless a pleasant way of doing a bit of true armchair modelling while simultaneously soaking up the atmosphere of the steam railway in its heyday more than half a century ago. Indeed, the more atmosphere you can absorb and subsequently replicate on your railway, the more accurate, satisfying and rewarding the hobby becomes.

IMPROVING THE APPEARANCE OF THE WAGON FLEET

It is now time to look at some simple ways of improving the overall appearance of the chosen working. This is best achieved by getting the individual wagons to seem as 'railway-like' as possible and wholly convincing, even when viewed in relative close-up.

The modeller who has space for only a small branch-line terminus will have little need to reproduce

This aerial view is perhaps typical of the way most of us actually watch our trains. This Manor-hauled working once again demonstrates just how much variety can be glimpsed in one rake of through-vans.

Express parcels are another excuse to run a wide variety of stock in one train, including larger bogie-vans, six-wheelers and passenger full-brakes. All the vehicles would be rated as 'XP' and can therefore run on your layouts at the same speeds as the passenger trains.

The overnight parcels trains often conveyed the railway's own traffic from its major stations or works to furthermost outposts. This is the nightly van from Swindon nearing its destination in the West Country.

the lengthy coal train or class C express vans. All that is required is the humble 'pick-up' branch goods. More fortunate enthusiasts, however, who may already be well on the way to a continuous-run main line, perhaps with extensive loops or relief lines, should find that all the workings described are a possibility. There are still, though, some constants that should be observed in nearly every case. It is then up to each individual to determine how best these might be accomplished and included in the layout's operations.

The main constant, of course, is the actual appearance of each vehicle. It is immaterial if they then combine into a lengthy train, or a mere half dozen or so trundle up and down a branch, or a few are seen standing in the goods yard. Every wagon must look right (railway-like and prototypical) whether viewed on its own in a siding or rattling past in the middle of a rake of express vans. The following notes and the accompanying illustrations will, I hope, prove to be useful. Incidentally, I like

This is my interpretation of that earlier photogaph of a 47xx with a lengthy train of mostly sheeted-opens. The '47' is a second-hand white-metal kit version. Its weight means that it can haul even the longest and heaviest workings with comparative ease.

to combine any weathering exercises with a periodic vehicle check and general service. There is little point in getting them to look right if they are poor runners due to dirty or out-of-gauge wheels and misaligned couplings. It is simple to set up a yard of track close to your worktable to check for 'levels' and, by raising one end a fraction, to make sure they run properly.

It is quite common to see the terms wear and tear and weathering combined under 'weathering'. However, I would advise separating them since they have different causes and produce different results.

The term wear and tear is applied to all the things that can happen to a wagon or van during its lifetime resulting from regular day-to-day use or misuse. It can take the form of nothing more than the polished centres of the buffers or the chipped and shiny appearance of hinges and latches. At the other end of the scale can be found broken or replaced planks, leaking roofs covered with a tarpaulin, new paintwork applied to coat a repair, chalked instructions adorning a van or simply material left over from previous loads.

Weathering, as its name suggests, covers the combined effects of rain and sun, of mileages covered, of oil stains and brake dust, soot and grime. All of these overlay, to a greater or lesser degree, the primary effects of wear and tear.

The best advice that is ever given to any modeller is to study the prototype and we have already identified the value of research. Railway modellers have one big advantage over those tackling military or aviation subjects in scales similar to our own. Our models are specifically created to move, not just sit on a plinth awaiting minute scrutiny. I will go even further and state that bigger layouts, more frequent operations, more rapid movements and a broader perspective of the whole scene reduce the need for microscopic detailing. The corollary, of course, is that smaller or branch-line layouts invite and make possible much closer inspection. As a result somewhat greater effort needs to be invested in all the finished models.

This is not intended to be a definitive exposition on the subject. There are literally scores of maga-

Not all goods trains were pulled by dirty looking engines. The newly built Standards were emerging from the various works and, typically, this one has gone straight into traffic on the 'Fawley Oil'. Note the requisite pair of empty open barrier-wagons at the front (vacuum-braked, of course). There is a similar pair at the back, since these were 'block workings' with the engine and brake-van simply swapping ends.

In a further attempt to recreate one of the archive images seen earlier, my H15 is here seen hauling an empty ballast train. This small class could be found with considerable design differences, so I have simply created my own hybrid. The boiler is from a long-scrapped Airfix Schools kit, the fittings are equally ancient white-metal parts, the cab and other parts are scratch-built from plastic sheet and the mechanism is from an Eastern Region B1 – and the tender should really go behind a Lord Nelson.

zine and textbook articles on the subject, many of which describe how to achieve optimum results by airbrushing or using the many expensive specialist powders and paints. If these represent a search for 'perfection', what follows may be taken as producing results that are 'acceptable'. The methods described are also quick, easy and inexpensive, requiring a limited investment of both time and money. The mediums used will be no more than those described in Chapter 1. With a modicum of practice even the most inexperienced of modellers should be able to treat several vehicles, if not a whole train, in a couple of evenings.

WOODEN-BODIED OPENS

These are by far the most common type throughout the period and are needed in a ratio of at least three to one (if not five to one) compared with vans

and other wagons. They belong in two groups: private owner and former company or BR stock. They are easily acquired off-the-shelf either as ready-to-run models or in kit form. If budgets are tight, they may be found second-hand at toy fairs. Except for examples from the Peco Wonderful Wagons series, these will have plastic bodies with a semi-gloss or satin finish and will boast accurate and well executed livery details. As bought they are certainly pretty, but that does not make them very 'railway-like'. Most real wagons during the period were pretty decrepit and long overdue for scrapping, despite the fact that the fleet still numbered several hundred thousand.

Wear and tear

The following steps will show how they can be quickly transformed. Always try to work on at least half a dozen wagons at a time.

This lengthy coal train for the west has an ROD in front, a typical locomotive for this sort of work. They were built in the First World War, at the instigation of the Ministry of Munitions, and were often nicknamed 'Maggie Murphys', or simply 'Maggies'. Those that survived by the 1950s had become pretty rough, although they were still quite strong. Many crews reckon they had just three speeds: 'Twenty miles-an-hour forwards, twenty miles-an-hour backwards and twenty miles-an-hour up and down!'

Underframes: Make sure that all the shiny plastic is covered. Extract the wheel sets and put to one side for reinsertion or for replacement with better metal versions, if necessary. Paint everything, including the solebars and buffers, with a matt black, preferably opting for a shade described as 'worn black', anthracite or very dark grey. The important factor is to ensure it is 'dead matt'.

Bodies: Even though we will be applying additional paint and other substances, these will not completely obliterate the gloss or semi-satin factory finish. I frequently resort to an aerosol can of Humbrol matt varnish (or similar) wafted lightly over the entire body. This is another good reason for working on a batch of vehicles. Next, select a range of matt wood-

toned enamels, or acrylics if you are happier with those. I suggest at least three or four, ranging from the near-cream of new timbers to a dark greeny-black for the older stuff. Note that I have refrained from specifying precise colours. We all perceive colour differently and each manufacturer also has its own interpretations. With the whole batch of wagons laid on their sides and end-to-end, simply work along them picking out individual groups of planks for treatment. It doesn't matter if your paint colours mix on the brush, indeed these subtle variations will actually improve things. Once this first exercise is complete, repeat the operation on the other side and on both ends. There are obviously no fixed rules for how many or how few planks should be treated. To provide variety, treat some as in slightly better condi-

These returning coal-empties are plodding up the snow-covered Winterbourne bank. Their Mogul will be going considerably more slowly than the one in the archive photograph shown earlier.

tion, with fewer replacements, and others in a more dilapidated condition.

Unless you intend the wagon to be sheeted or bulk loaded, carry out a similar operation on the insides, paying special attention to the wagon bed (floor). Finally, attend to the various bits of ironwork, such as the strapping, hinges, latches and chains, with a very fine brush,. Some will be rusty, some just worn, while other bits may well have had a repaint. Whatever you do is entirely up to you. You can now show a bit of wear and tear on the underframes, suggesting just a little judicious rust here and there and some evidence of contacts on the centre of the buffers. This latter need be no more than a spot of Metalcote steel or aluminium: avoid 'silver' as it doesn't look right.

One final item often neglected but essential on post-war wagons is the application of a small black patch on the bottom left-hand corner of all wagon sides. This should be roughly 12in (4mm or two planks) deep by about 18in (6mm). Once dry, inscribe the letter 'P' and a long wagon number with a mapping pen and white ink. This was applied to all commandeered private owner wagons during the war and it remained in place until the vehicle was scrapped. Unless the stock is going to be viewed close up, a few squiggles will probably give a quite acceptable result.

Weathering

It is now time to reach to reach for the pastels. I suggest using a range from greyish white, dull grey/greens and various brownish rusts, to dark greys. Even black can be applied if the wagon has been used for coal. Using an emery board, create small heaps of pastel dust on the chosen palette ready for application. Since this is a dusty operation, I would advise working on a sheet of newspaper. There are no fixed rules about where the various

This 14xx, with its three-wagon trip-freight, is shown on the author's other layout based on the old Didcot, Newbury and Southampton Junction Railway, which now provides much of the route of the A34. The forge in the background, which still stands opposite the village pond in Childrey, belonged to my father.

colours should be applied, but you should constantly refer to selected photos from your colour albums or magazines for guidance. The pastel dusts can be applied with soft watercolour brushes, cotton buds, tissues, paint sponges or even fingertips. The golden rule is to apply relatively small amounts, building up the coverage and the densities almost layer by layer. The 'rust' colours should be applied only to the metal surfaces, such as the underframe and the wagon strapping, while dusty greys may be applied everywhere. As a general rule the darker shades and more dense coverings should be confined to cracks and crevices; they are also more pronounced on the corners, lower regions and wagon ends. Working in batches helps to ensure that there is an essential uniformity of overall appearance within the rake, and eventually within the whole train. No single wagon should stand out, unless it represents an example of a new BR-built item with no wear and tear and merely a hint of newly acquired grime.

VANS

Most of the vans of this period were former Big Four company vehicles. There were a few private owner examples, but many of these were more recent additions to the fleet. Indeed, a large number of the model r-t-r private owner vans are most definitely post-war examples. It is worth noting that the very nature of van traffic and the cargoes that it carried meant that it was less subject to the harsh everyday treatment meted out to its open counterparts.

Wear and tear

There is only limited photographic evidence of re-planking. Treat the vans in the same way as opens. Use matt varnish on the bodies and most definitely the roofs to kill any shine. Apply matt blacks and greys to the underframe. Pick out a few planks across the batch, but definitely not on every vehicle. The area most likely requiring repair would be the doors and then it would probably be to the planks nearest the hinges and latches. It is almost certain that such a repair would have received a coat or two of paint in the original grey or brown of its former livery. For our period the roofs should be predominantly black or dark grey and, again, absolutely matt. To introduce variety, and prototypical accuracy, it is worth modelling a few vans with leaking roofs covered by tarpaulins. The latter can be sourced from the paper versions of company sheets within the Roger Smith range. Most photographs, however, show nondescript, unbranded tarpaulins in the typically washed-out greens, browns and blacks of the period. I find that the thinnest sandwich bags cut to size make a useful starting point. These should be stretched out taut on the cutting mat and secured with masking tape before being painted with appropriate matt enamels and cut to size. Once on the van they need to be well roped down, so they are best left off until all the other treatments have been completed. Many vans would be covered with the chalk hieroglyphics relating to loads, dates and

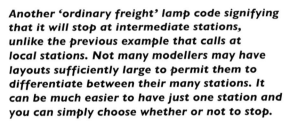

Another 'ordinary freight' lamp code signifying that it will stop at intermediate stations, unlike the previous example that calls at local stations. Not many modellers may have layouts sufficiently large to permit them to differentiate between their many stations. It can be much easier to have just one station and you can simply choose whether or not to stop.

The demand for steel was almost as great in the 1950s as it had been during the war. Most 'mixed goods' would have a couple of wagons and complete trains, as here, were not uncommon. My loads display the careful hoarding of metal detritus from decades of kit and figure construction, augmented by bits of broken plastic kits. Several wagons are filled with rust-painted wheels left over from replacement tasks. The engine is another ROD carrying the short-lived, red-backed BR number plate.

destinations. Use a mapping pen and white ink to reproduce these, varying the clarity and density, and always include some crossings-out.

Weathering

Follow the same principles and procedures described above for the opens. Van planking styles can vary, however, and the concentration of dust and dirt at the corners and lower areas seems more pronounced. Van bodies are one area where you can quite effectively use a short cut. Instead of applying pastel dust, several dustings of talcum powder can be used in the same way. This is excellent for toning down the whole vehicle. Talcum will also work on the roofs, but here I prefer to use a dark blueish-grey pastel to give the necessary soft sooty effect. Once the bodies of the selected models are finished you can add any tarpaulins. Glue them on to the roofs and eaves with PVA. Finally, following the available photo references, fix securing ropes made from suitable thread to the sheet and to the appropri-

ate fixing points on the solebar. You should make sure that, as with the opens, the batch of vans achieves the correct overall uniformity across the rake while maintaining the subtle differences of each individual vehicle. All of these comments apply equally to vans of all types, ranging from unbraked four-wheelers to the large bogie vehicles that would normally run as 'non-passenger carriage-stock'. Remember that each of those variations requires its own treatment: some types of four-wheel wooden vans had horizontal planking, for example, while others had metal ends, were all metal or had sides of plain plywood.

TANK WAGONS

Tank wagons for transporting milk, oils or petroleum are among the most obvious examples of the type. The r-t-r manufacturers have produced models in almost every prototype livery. At the time, however, these liveries were barely discern-

These cattle wagons, shown paused for a routine 'feed and water' stop, display some typical variations in livery, detailing and weathering. Wagons constructed with vacuum brakes should always be coupled next to the engine to produce a 'fitted head', which permitted shorter journey times.

ible on the 'daily milk' or the 'block oil' under all the glutinous grime. In all my years as a spotter – or the time since spent examining photographs – I have never come across the shiny white milk trains much loved by modellers. Smart silver or glossy black oil tanks were almost as rare. Some work is definitely needed to ensure that r-t-r items even halfway resemble the railway-like everyday appearance of their prototypes. This is truly a subject where desk research comes into its own.

Before you even reach for a paintbrush, search out as many colour images as you can and keep them close to hand while you work.

One thing you may notice is that the real wagons appear to have more securing straps than the models. This will certainly be true of the old Dublo-Wrenn six-wheel milk tanks and they are not the only offenders. These omissions can be rectified by using the thinnest possible 1mm wide plastic strip secured to the tanks with liquid poly and to the

The author's usual workbench for weathering and stock servicing. When not in use it is simply pushed back beneath the layout. When doing these jobs, always ensure you work under a really good light (a bulb with a daylight colour temperature is a sound investment). Note the stock drawer for the meat-train and the small, but vital, back-to-back gauge: 14.5mm is the ideal general purpose measurement.

solebars with a dab of cyano. You should also check that your examples carry the proper vacuum-brake standards. Even then the tanks will still have to be extensively and sensibly painted. Most of the visible surfaces will need to be covered; only those that normally remain unseen should probably be left untouched. This effectively means there is no need for the initial matt respray and you can start at once with the enamels, acrylics and 'dirty thinners', finishing with the pastels. The most significant examples of weathering and usage will show on the tops of the tanks as a result of spillage when loading; spillage in transit should not occur. The stains and general muck will flow downwards over the tanks to a point along the lower half where gravity causes most of it to drip off. Your palette should include the obvious matt blacks, greys and browns. You could perhaps apply metallic black on the oil tanks to show the iridescent shine of more recent deposits. Most of the work can be done with a broad brush, always dragging the paint downwards. Careful study of photographs will reveal what is required with greater clarity than any verbal description. Finish off with pastel dust to the underframes and steelwork. As in the previous examples, it will pay to work in batches to ensure consistency across the rake.

OTHER TYPES

This general section covers a wide range of types – ancient cattle trucks, steel-bodied non-passenger carriage stock, the whole range of steel mineral wagons, flats, well wagons and bolsters – together with their modern BR replacement stock. Cattle trucks can be treated in an appropriate blend of the applications for both wagons and vans. Replacement planks to the corner sections were commonplace, since cows kick! Horseboxes and the wide variety of metal vans and parcel/full brakes can be treated as carriage stock, although they were much less frequently cleaned. Some can be matt-sprayed, while others can simply rely on pastel treatment. Roofs and underframes will need the full procedures used for vans.

Although the underframes of steel-bodied open wagons can be dealt with in the same way as everything else, the bodies need to be treated differently. We can quickly dispose of the more unusual wagons like wells and bolsters as they will need little more than the usual dulling down. There will also be accumulations of dust and debris on their many flat surfaces, coils of rope, chains and old timbers dumped between loads. Signs of chipping and rust will be evident on the painted sections. Steel-bodied minerals, including the very few branded private owner vehicles,

A length of track on a suitable batten is a sure way of quickly checking for any faults with couplings and the general 'ride and roll' qualities of your stock. These meat vans are now ready to rejoin the others. A simple piece of card or paper will help your examinations.

This fine example of how a former private owner wagon would look in the early days of British Railways demonstrates what we have lost as colour film was so scarce in those years. Nonetheless it shows all too clearly just how far you can go with 'wear and tear' and weathering.
STEAM MUSEUM OF THE GREAT WESTERN RAILWAY, SWINDON

A selection of the author's open wagons. None of them has taken more than a few minutes to 'weather' using blends of enamels, watercolours and pastels, and without needing an airbrush. They may not look perfect in absolute close-up, and are far removed from the exquisite examples made by masters of the craft, but they appear more than sufficiently 'railway-like' on the layout.

will show dents and bulges on the larger panels, together with much chipping and rust elsewhere. It is no exaggeration to say that some of the more advanced modellers have taken these aspects of weathering beyond an art form into the realms of a near-science. Nonetheless, it is possible to capture their true 'railway-like' appearance using the most rudimentary of techniques. The bodies will require dulling down, but this is less essential than on wooden stock since their painted metal will be slower to show signs of ageing. Once again good colour photos will reveal your targeted finish.

Early photographs of cattle trucks show the interiors to have been limewashed, with considerable spillage apparent on the exteriors as well. I have noticed that this practice has been replicated on a number of layouts set in the 1950s. I am sorry to have to report that this came to an end in the 1930s, at the very latest.

SPECIALIST VEHICLES

By their very definition, these will be far fewer in number than the vans and, even more so, than the opens. They will also be of very different construction and therefore show the effects of time and usage in different ways. The best advice I can offer is to search out appropriate colour photographs and use these as your reference.

Read the Small Print

Something that most people forget is that, as well as the routine halts for livestock trains, all goods workings were regularly halted for wheel and axle-box examinations. As a general rule vacuum trains with modern boxes were stopped every 115 miles (185km), while ordinary trains with largely grease axle-boxes could only do 50 miles (80km) between stops. The job would be done by a checker, accompanied by an assistant carrying the box of grease. The train would be held on a loop or refuge siding and the pair would then walk the length, up one side and back the other. Any faulty wagons identified would be cut out and left for repair or load transfer. This would make an intriguing operation to replicate on your layout, especially as many exhibition visitors would remain baffled by the stop and the two 'huminiatures' in overalls beside the track. Railway modelling, after all, resembles any other hobby or pursuit in that the rewards are in proportion to the effort put into it.

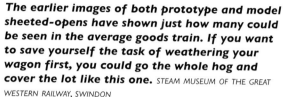

The earlier images of both prototype and model sheeted-opens have shown just how many could be seen in the average goods train. If you want to save yourself the task of weathering your wagon first, you could go the whole hog and cover the lot like this one. *STEAM MUSEUM OF THE GREAT WESTERN RAILWAY, SWINDON*

An excellent example of a repaired wood-planked van. Not all of those in service would have been quite so patched-up. There are no hard and fast rules about how many you should treat or to what extent: perhaps a fifth might show modest repairs and a tenth might be on their last legs, like this much-abused relic. *STEAM MUSEUM OF THE GREAT WESTERN RAILWAY, SWINDON*

Both kit-built and r-t-r wagons run happily together on 'Wessex Lines'. It is, however, almost impossible to assemble realistic van workings without recourse to the kit market: and remember the earlier examples with leaking roofs. This is a quick way of adding interest to your trains and still keeping faith with the prototype.

The various types of tank wagons usually need more work with enamels that are both variously thinned and straight from the tin due to their rounded profiles. It is not unrealistic to completely obscure the original livery details. As is suggested by the state of the Plymouth–Kensington working earlier in this chapter, I would go so far as to say that this is all but essential on milk tanks.

CHAPTER THREE

THE GOODS SHED

GOODS SHEDS ON THE REAL RAILWAY

The humble goods shed was a key feature at almost every station: the only likely exceptions were at the extreme ends of the scale, where major urban termini were served by vast depots, while humble wayside halts often had no buildings at all. Their size and scope would originally reflect the aspirations of the parent company for that precise location. In most cases the mid-Victorian entrepreneurs predicted their needs accurately and the sheds remained largely unaltered. There were instances, however, where nearly everything would arrive by rail, and industrial demands developing on the back of the railway soon outstripped the existing facilities. In response to these changes, some sheds were simply extended while others had new covered accommodation tacked on to the original structures. Irrespective of their relative size and scope, their purpose was always to provide a covered and secure facility for the loading, offloading and temporary storage of vulnerable cargo.

At their most simple this could take the form of a separate structure built either on the passenger platform or located somewhere convenient in the goods yard. These were not rail served in the true sense of the word and required the various items to be manhandled to and from the shed between the customer and the railway. While they have no real place in the subsequent chapters, they are worth bearing in mind as additional facilities to the goods shed proper. There are many examples across the

Swanage shed is an excellent example of how the coming of the railway quickly boosted industry and commerce to such an extent that it soon needed to be extended to twice its original size. Its roadside access was increased from a single entrance to three.

Corfe shed, also on the Swanage branch, was made from locally sourced Purbeck stone, quarried only a few miles away.

The shed is one of the smaller types without a through track. Corfe will be discussed in more detail in Chapter 6 when it will be the subject of a scratch-building project.

UK where private companies generating considerable rail traffic built their own storage sheds within the yard. Agricultural companies like R. Silcock & Sons often had their own provender stores for fertilizers, seeds and animal feed, which would arrive in bulk by the vanload and then be held awaiting delivery or collection by their individual customers.

Returning to the sheds themselves, the next type to be considered are those without a covered 'through road'. These would be located at smaller wayside or branch stations that would expect to handle only a few vanloads a week. They would be located in the goods yard with one side providing access to a siding or loop and the other giving vehicle access for wagons and lorries. Some were quite substantial stone or brick structures while others, especially on more impecunious systems, were little more than tin or timber-built shacks. Nonetheless they would all have secure doors on both sides, most often the sliding type, and nearly all protected by suitable canopies. The interiors would be simply one large 'platform', usually timber built and

lacking in any equipment apart from the obligatory weighing scales and sack trucks, and perhaps a small office for the checker.

The commonest form of shed, and the ones that will be featured in the following sections, are those with fully covered rail access either by a siding or a goods loop. These varied enormously in size, scope and construction and could handle anything from a couple of vans to larger buildings handling perhaps half a dozen. Viewed at their most simple they would have a plain, windowed wall facing the railway. The rail line entered and exited via the gable ends, fitted with opening or sliding doors to secure the entrances. The shed itself had a full-length platform (or dock) running right across the interior to the roadside wall; this would have one or more large securable doorways for vehicle loading and offloading. The interior equipment would depend upon the size of the shed, but could include cranes and transverse hoists capable of 30cwt loads (1.5 tonnes), various scales, sack trucks or trollies, and perhaps a checker's desk.

The goods shed at Dunster on the West Somerset Railway is another example using local stone. It gives it a unique character that is very different from the previous examples.

In most cases the checker's office would be a separate extension on the outside of the shed itself. This could be a simple small office with a couple of windows and the obligatory open fire and chimney stack. At larger sheds these facilities could well run to a two-storey extension, with a proper gable-end roof, and maybe even a toilet. In all cases these offices would be built as an integral part of the main building and would blend in using the same materials and architectural design.

I would find it hard to decide whether brick or stone were more commonly used. On balance, the determining factor was probably whichever material was the most economical and commonly available within each area.

This presents a challenge for the modeller, especially when using kits from different manufacturers or the newer 'ready to site' models. It is desirable that the shed should always be built of the same materials and in the architectural style used for all the other station buildings, including the construction of the platform and docks.

The actual working of these goods sheds was mostly consistent across the country. The main variables were the amount of traffic processed and the proportions and ratios of that traffic. The latter would depend upon the predominance, or otherwise, of any particular industry. Some parts of the country might handle woollens with bulk bundles inbound and more carefully packaged finished goods outbound. Similar examples could include electricals, furniture, brewing or agriculture any of which would dominate all the other commercial or personal consignments.

As a general rule the more perishable, vulnerable or valuable consignments would be more likely to transit through the goods shed. Even in these cases it would not necessarily entail van traffic. A vast amount of cargo and merchandise always travelled in sheeted-opens and these, as with the vans, did not have to comprise vacuum-braked stock. Loose-coupled wagons and vans handled the bulk of wagonload traffic right up until the end of steam.

On the road side, the shed would be the delivery and collection point for all manner of vehicles. At

The shed at Dunster is stoutly built and has decorative quoins and elaborate arched windows.

The small goods office can be accessed only through the shed building. Note the massive wooden doors securing the rail entrance; an even larger pair protect the shed at the road entrance.

Further along the line, the bigger shed at Williton is built in a similar style and from the same local stone. Note that the south gable end here has a planked finish.

The roadside doors are of the sliding type, but the overall character and appearance resembles that of most of the structures on this popular tourist line.

the beginning of the chosen period this could well include a lorry still in the livery of one of the old 'Big Four' companies. These would be quickly replaced by British Railways' own 'crimson and cream' fleet accompanied by the red or green nationalized vehicles of British Road Services. Alongside these, there is always an excuse for run-down ex-military trucks used by the local farmers. There were also pre-war flat beds or vans still in private hands and the somewhat smarter modern removal vans of local or national

contractors. In rural areas horse-drawn carts or a tractor and trailer would be frequent visitors.

In summary then, the humble goods shed provides opportunities for constantly changing scenes on both rail and road sides. If you intend to operate through trains with the goods shed simply acting as a scenic feature, you could always imagine that it is evening or a Sunday, and model the shed with all its doors firmly shut and road traffic conspicuous by its absence.

MODELLING GOODS SHEDS

THE AVAILABLE OPTIONS

When it comes to recreating the goods shed in card model form, the choice of kits is much wider than it might seem. Most stockists will generally have ample supplies from the two best-known manufacturers: Superquick and Metcalf. It is appropriate that they are featured in the building projects that follow.

That is not the end of the story, however, as some specialist stockists and manufacturers are able to supply kits, often in updated versions, that are no longer readily available on the high street. There are also many newer companies who make excellent use of the internet and of the steadily improving results of printed downloads via a home computer.

At the time of writing (late 2013) there are nine goods sheds currently available. Although none of these less common versions will be selected for the projects, several will be illustrated. This should help demonstrate what can be obtained by the modeller who is prepared to hunt around before buying. In the following sections we will examine how even

these can be further customized to better reflect the layout's location.

As a general rule a goods shed can face either way, depending upon your normal operating position. The best way round is to have the road access side facing the viewer. The other side is, of course, little more than a large wall with a few windows. The preferred side not only lets you position road vehicles for loading or unloading, it also allows you a view of the interior, or at least a partial one, with the obvious potential for even more detailed modelling.

It would appear that most goods sheds had a through road to enable wagons and vans to be dealt with completely under cover. Certainly the kits on the market favour this type. They will be our starting point.

The two most popular versions naturally come from the two premier names in card kits: Superquick and Metcalf. Read any model railway magazine or visit any exhibition and the chances are that one, or both, of these versions will appear on the featured layouts. More recently, however, the improvements in computer and printer technology have introduced further options. Scalescenes, for example, offers reasonably priced downloads of pre-printed kits that are good value, permit multiple free reprints and come with optional finishes.

Card kits produced by Superquick and Metcalf are available from high street stockists, specialist model shops or by mail order.

This original Prototype kit of Little Bytham goods shed on the former LNER has been given extra detailing, including the new and appropriate valancing, and repainted into the correct Southern Region buff. It now blends with the adjacent station buildings, which have been similarly treated.

This Prototype kit, based on the small timber-built shed at Watlington in Oxfordshire, has been enhanced with a fully detailed interior, new roof lights and individually cut external planks.

This is probably the smallest item available in card-kit form. It comes from the well-known Alphagraphix range and is based on the version at Fairford. It is unusual in that the printed details are simply stone outlines for the modeller to paint as he chooses. On my 'East Ilsley' exhibition layout I covered the whole kit with brick paper to blend with the other buildings.

Over the next few pages we will assemble the Superquick and Metcalf kits as their manufacturers intended, albeit to the highest level possible. Since this book is all about making your railway truly your own, we will then see how they can be improved and customized to give them a more unique character. By the end of the chapter every modeller should have a goods shed that, if not an exact replica of an existing prototype, still looks authentic and fully at home in its chosen setting.

BUILDING AND DETAILING THE SUPERQUICK GOODS SHED

The Superquick range of kits has been around for a long time. Superquick was among the first companies to introduce pre-cut card models. The current offering is their second version, but even this has been available for decades rather than years. It is reasonably priced (currently retailing at about £7.00) and it remains a popular starting point for many modellers. It is not based on any particular example, nor does it

show much relationship to any of the major railway companies, but it is well suited to the beginner.

Its low cost, however, comes at the expense of a lack of authenticity and certain defects in its design and actual assembly. One of its most obvious design deficiencies is the lack of doors to the rail entrances. The external loading dock is useful, but it is 'white lined' all round, implying that it should be rail served on both sides and also via its end dock. This is all very well, except that goods platforms were rarely, if ever, white lined (a wartime addition to passenger stations during the blackout), the dock should be a 'rail to road' interface, not 'rail to rail', and the end dock can't work since there is no access for vehicles to the dock. I also have doubts about the apparent asphalt or paving block platform inside. In my experience most were heavyweight wooden board floors. The final mistake is the ramped external platform leading to the small entrance door to the interior of the shed. It is hard to see any purpose for this apart from the very occasional need for a porter to wheel a sack truck up into the shed.

The starting point for the Superquick shed. It looks relatively straightforward, but care is needed when separating the various components. Make sure you have a new blade in your scalpel or craft knife.

From an assembly point of view it can be tricky to work on. The instructions are mainly in running text and there are few illustrations. They need to read, and re-read, several times with the two fretted card sheets close at hand in order to identify the various components.

That said, I suspect that most modellers will then determine their own procedural path to get to the final build. The instructions recommend PVA adhesive, which I would certainly endorse, but would further advise keeping a contact adhesive handy for the glazing. They also advise you, again wisely, to use watercolours to disguise the exposed joints, but I disagree with their recommendation to paint these before assembly. It is much better to leave this until the job is complete so that you can see exactly where the paints are needed. One final point, especially for those who are perhaps more familiar with the precise fit of plastic kits, is that you may need to offer up the components several times to check which way round ensures the best fit for square or vertical. You will also need to raid the odd piece from other kits or add extra support. The captions to the accompanying photographs should clarify these points.

This is not intended to sound negative, since, the kit makes a quite acceptable and inexpensive shed after a bit of perseverance. By paying attention to the finish and adding a few improvements, we can certainly enhance it and still stay short of a more major transformation. Note that I have also shown how to make the roof detachable to permit any necessary work on the interior. All the small tasks shown have obviously been carried out on the finished model, largely for the benefit of those who already have similar 'as bought' versions on their layouts. It goes without saying that some improvements are both easier and quicker to carry out during the actual assembly processes.

The main components in the course of assembly.

The loading dock, access ramp and office are complete and the main shell can now be put together. This is probably the best time to add any interior details, if desired.

The basic box is briefly taped up. This is the time to check that everything is square, upright and fits snugly. It is also an opportunity to offer it up on the layout or track-plan to make sure it fits.

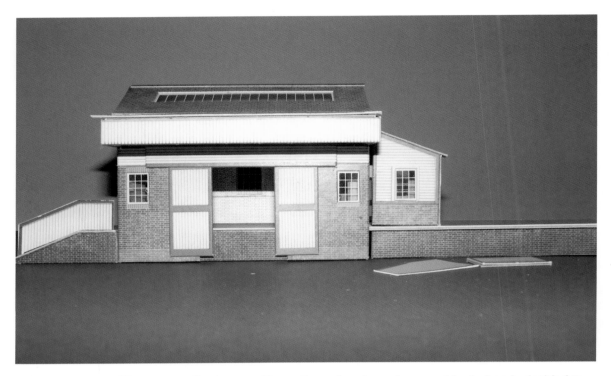

ABOVE AND BELOW: *The apparently spare sections of woodwork are because I had already decided to remodel the entrance ramp. Even without flash photography the inevitable 'shine from the printed surfaces is all too obvious.*

Simple improvements

All of these tasks fall into the quick and easy category, but together they help to make the most of what is a comparatively basic kit.

Scribing the woodwork is a relatively quick exercise, but it does demand an element of concentration and accuracy. Use a steel ruler as a guide and a scalpel or craft knife with a sharp blade. Lightly score all the vertical planking on the doors, including the edges of the brown frames, and do the same on the canopy valence. This will help disguise the regularity of the printing and will add a little relief detail, especially for when it comes to the weathering process.

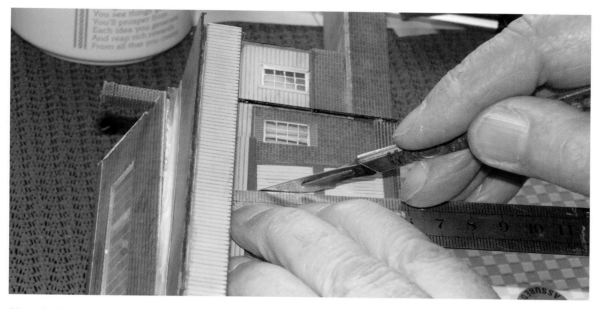

The planking can be scribed at any convenient stage in the construction. In these two examples the building has been completed to demonstrate that it can be carried out quite easily on a finished model.

The interior of the model really needs to have a wooden floor. This is made from balsa strip, which is very easy to cut and can be fixed with PVA. Run the 'planks' vertically, that is from rail edge back to the wall. An alternative might be to use coffee stirrers, although these need a bit more effort to cut.

I chose to discard the pointless ramped entry to the doorway and instead built up a simple flight of steps using the kit's fencing as a template.

The external loading dock can be improved by covering the surface either with handmade paving slabs or using a section from any one of the available pre-printed sheets. I chose to use Superquick Grey Pavement and so made it consistent with any other paved areas in the goods yard. Remember to remove the unnecessary overhang where the dock butts up against the shed's gable end.

I replaced the totally inappropriate ramped access to the outer doorway with a flight of steps cut from balsa strip. The loading dock was covered with Superquick paving in an effort to hide the unwarranted white-lined platform edges.

I was not at all together happy with the windows as supplied, since their yellow glazing bars are plainly wrong. There is little that one can do to the finished model, so the best answer is to replace them during assembly. If that is not possible you could try to improve them in-situ using either drawing ink with a mapping pen or, although it is quite expensive, a Rapidograph.

We should now turn our attention to the kit's lack of an office chimney. Most card kits present these small chimney stacks as four-sided fold-overs with a fixing tab. In this case, however, I recommend the use of a solid wood former covered with the nearest available match of printed brick paper. Unfortunately my closest matching paper was significantly different, so I took the easy way out and decided that the office was a later addition and therefore justified re-bricking the whole lower portion to match the chimney. The cap can be either a cut-out square of thickish card or balsa wood;

Just as the scribing can be done at any stage, so can the job of painting or detailing the various glazing bars. These tasks, though, will demand a very steady hand and a firmly held structure to avoid the risk of any wobbles.

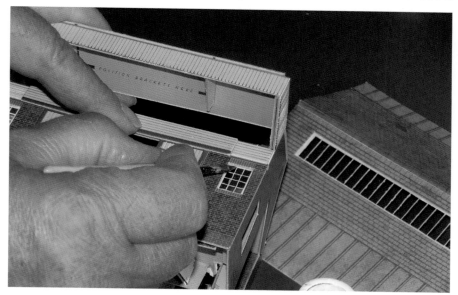

I fabricated a chimney to keep the goods porter from freezing to death in the winter, replacing the office tiling and improving the brickwork at the same time.

ABOVE AND OPPOSITE: *The intended position for the office on the loading dock exposes a weakness of the design. The dock itself would appear to be served by rail on both sides, meaning that there is no access for potential visitors to the office except by leaping onto the platform. Observe that the rail entrance doors are now in place at both ends.*

alternatively you could use a small lump of plasticine moulded to shape. The chimney pot can be cut from a cotton wool bud of suitable dimensions pressed or glued into place on the chosen cap.

Finally we come to some basic painting, including the disguising of any exposed joins. The interior, apart from the side walls, is plain dark card. Using off-white matt enamel, acrylic or emulsion paint,

cover all the exposed surfaces including the undersides of the roof and canopy. (Avoid using too much paint, as wet cardboard will buckle and distort.) The same paint can be used on the timbered loading dock, but add some darker greys and browns around the walls to show the lesser amounts of wear and tear. Once this is dry, select a fine detailing brush to apply watercolours to

those exposed edges. Don't be too dismayed if you cannot get a true match. Watercolour on absorbent card will never look the same as shiny printing ink. Inevitably a lot of trial and error is involved: I would suggest test applications on less visible areas before carefully touching in the exposed portions.

Once these tasks have been completed the model is ready to be weathered and bedded into its chosen site on the layout. You may, however, choose to explore an intermediate stage that falls short of the more major customizing described later.

Adding extra detail

This next section takes us a step further into the world of real modelling. None of it is particularly complex and no task should take more than an hour or so at the most. There are about half a dozen little jobs that all contribute to a more authentic structure. These include double doors to the two rail entrances; a relief plinth around the base; barge-boards and weatherboards for the roof; drainpipes and guttering; an interior hoist; loads and clutter on the loading docks; and internal roof detailing (only where visible through the roof lights and entrances).

Doors: These are easier to install fully open, but a bit of ingenuity involving small hinges might enable them to be properly closed at night and week-ends. They are quite massive structures and should reflect this in their construction. Dimensionally each of the four doors should be 56mm (14ft) high and 20mm (5ft) wide, solidly planked on the outside and with stout frames on the inside. Probably the best material to use is the scrap card off the back of an A4 pad or similar.

Draw out all the four doors as a single workpiece. Mark the vertical planks on both sides, then lightly score them with a scalpel or craft knife. Separate them and lay them face down, so that the insides are ready to be detailed. Cut some lengths of card 3mm wide and some more 2mm wide: these will represent the frames and cross members. Using PVA, glue the two 56 x 3mm vertical frames to the edges of each of the four doors. The horizontal frames, each approximately 14 x 3mm, are added across the top, bottom and centre of all doors. The 'X' shape reinforcing members are made of 2mm strip cut for a snug fit, with a 45-degree point at each end. Glue the first reinforcement member (say top left to bottom right) above and below the centre cross members. Let them dry thoroughly before taking the last strips and cutting them in half, remembering to shorten each half by 1mm. These should be glued bottom right to top left to complete the 'X' shapes. Prime both sides of the doors with white enamel or emulsion and leave to dry. When drying, but still pliable, place them beneath a pile of books to ensure they harden off completely flat. Once this is done, paint the insides white (to match the interior) and the outsides in whichever mix you have chosen to match the pre-printed cream/yellow woodwork. The doors can then be hung – glued – in the open position, parallel to the track, with their tops flush to the top of the entrance and ensuring that they clear the top of the rails at the bottom. Finally cut three hinge shapes from the card and glue them along the cross members with the butt of the hinges glued to the shed walls. These can be touched in with white, or with black, if you want them to stand out.

Plinth: The model features a pre-printed non-relief plinth of five courses of engineer's blue bricks. This should be overlaid with a deeper relief strip that has at least seven courses. Engineer's blue brick was often used decoratively as well as structurally, and this is always a useful brick paper to have to hand. Cut the required plinth lengths (of the chosen depth) from the same scrap card used for the doors. Using ordinary paper glue, fix the pre-printed brick courses, turning the paper over the top edge to avoid any need for touching-in. Reverting to PVA, simply overlay the original pre-print with the new plinth. With care, and a subtle scoring to the inner side, it should be possible to avoid more butt joins on the corner and simply bend the card through the required right angle.

Barge-boards: The pre-printed barge-boards already on the kit are 3mm (scale 9in) deep and these should be replicated on the additions. Cut the required 3mm strips from good-quality white record cards (or similar) and glue them beneath the edge of the roof at both the gable ends. They should then be painted to match. The goods office can be embellished in the same way, but using thinner strips that are only 2mm (scale 6in) deep.

Drainpipes and guttering: Studying the model reveals that the only visible guttering would be on the far (rail side) wall and you might wonder whether it is worth bothering with. Drainpipes can be properly sited on each corner and will look more attractive if they feature a swan neck at the top receiving rainwater from an unseen gutter. When choosing from one of the several plastic accessory packs, the items selected should first be pre-painted with enamel, either in black or in the closest match to the printed woodwork. A smaller, but similar, installation is all that is needed for the goods office. Alternatives can be made up from suitable thicknesses of plastic rod or the heavier types of florist's wire. These can be further detailed by adding small slivers of Sellotape (approximately 2mm deep) wrapped around the wire at about 25mm intervals to represent the joints and mounting points.

Hoist or crane: This can be reproduced using one of the plastic kit hoists from Wills. This, though, is a rather fine little model and may be just too good for this purpose. A cheaper, but somewhat fiddly, alternative is to construct a track-to-doorway hoist across the centre of the shed. The version shown is no more than an inverted trough made from three thin hardwood strips with thin florist's wire as a guide inside the trough. Threaded on to this is a loop or two of fine chain with a small hook on the end. This can then be made into a more visible feature by adding an appropriate load being walked to the loading bay by a porter or perhaps in the act of being lowered onto a waiting lorry.

Loads and clutter: You do not need enough to fill the shed. A few sacks, barrels and boxes will suggest the activity well enough. The ones shown are a mixture of plasticine, modelling clay and oddments from the bits box, including crates and parcels.

With the roof subassembly put to one side, it is possible to fabricate and install a transverse hoist. If you wish, this could be extended to run beyond the edge of the dock and out beneath the canopy.

A van driver's eye view of the loading-dock, giving a brief glimpse of the hoist and some of the interior clutter.

Improving the roof

The overall design of the roof as it stands does not help anyone trying to make it removable. The projection over the canopy and rather strange flat portion over the rail-side wall are as unrealistic as they are unwieldy. The canopies with their apparently felt-covered roof should start from below the eaves of the main roof, or from a few slates up with the join protected by lead flashing. The purpose of the flat portion leaves me mystified. The best solution I can come up with is to separate these two elements and eventually glue them down as permanent fixtures.

Inner roof supports are a matter of choice. If the roof is to be detachable then any detailing should be fixed to its underside. If the roof is permanent, so that the whole building is lifted off to allow for any track cleaning, then the detail can be built up across the shed walls. This basic design is fairly straightforward

and can be easily assembled from balsa or hardwood strip. The photos should clarify the result of this exercise. I would stress that it is only worthwhile if the end product can be easily seen. Whichever option you choose, the starting point is the same and it does require some preparatory work.

Constructing the roof supports: First take a length of hardwood or balsa approximately $3/16$ x $1/32$in (5 x 1mm) deep and ensure it is a tight fit between the very tops of the gable ends, immediately below the eventual ridge line. Lightly glue it in place or secure with Blu-tack. Next take two thin strips of hardwood and similarly glue them lightly, or secure with Blu-tack, between the gable end walls at the height of the eaves. These two have no long term future for the removable roof but can otherwise be permanently glued. It's a question of judgement, but I think that two trusses

The revamped office and freshly paved dock are shown together with the new roof trusses and removable roof. The trusses, here still under construction, will be glued to the underside of the detachable roof when complete. If you are making a version with a fixed roof, the trusses could sit on the walls in the usual way.

each one-third of the way in are all that is needed. To build the 'triangle', use $^1/_{16}$in (2mm) balsa strip running first across the shed resting on the hardwood supports, then trim the further pieces to run from the top of these cross members to the ridge piece, and finally add a central upright and some extra bracing. The photos show the finished arrangement. All these last joints should be made permanent by using balsa cement. If the roof is to be permanently fixed, paint the trusses and then glue the roof and the two separated projections in place.

Removable roof: If the roof is to be removable, draw the outline of the gable ends on a piece of foamboard and cut them out with a sharp scalpel, ensuring that the tops of the cut are perfectly square. Offer up the roof and lightly mark the points where it rests on the inside walls. Glue the foamboard to the underside of the roof with the outer side exactly against those marks. This should make it a snug push fit. Offer up the roof once again and this time mark

the positions of the two trusses. Finally unstick the temporary fixings to the supports and carefully lift out the two trusses and the joining piece. Shorten the ridge piece to fit between the inner sides of foamboard, then glue this whole subassembly to the underside of the roof.

Completing the assembly: Glue the two separated roof sections (the canopy and the rail-side flat roof) into position and allow them to dry. The main roof, complete with trusses, can now be gently pushed into place. As a final touch, a small strip of thin paper can be glued along the bottom row of slates to overlap the canopy and flat roof by the same amount. This can be painted in silvery-grey to represent lead flashing and disguise the join. Lastly, fix the bargeboards beneath the gable ends of the roof; these will also hide away any small errors of fit between the walls and the roof. Paint any detailing extras such as drainpipes and then weather with pastels to achieve the best end product.

The view from below the detachable roof with the trusses now glued in place. Also seen here are the 5mm foamboard wedges, which are a push-fit between the gable ends.

Painting the added drainpipes is another job that can be left until the end, using ordinary black enamel or, if you can find some, the appropriate colours for your company or BR Region.

Patient, careful weathering adds the finishing touches. This is best applied with a soft watercolour brush. tissue, sponge, cotton-wool bud or your fingertip. Build up the effects gradually and simply blow away any excess.

CUSTOMIZING THE GOODS SHED

If the early parts of this chapter were given over to making the best of the basic Superquick goods shed, then what follows could be described as how to transform it completely. It is a logical intermediate step between kit building and scratch building, in that most of the techniques belong to the latter but the basic structure itself is provided by the kit.

The example shown uses an earlier version of the Superquick shed (in this case an ancient, poorly built and much neglected model priced at £2.00 at a toy fair), that offers the same opportunities for customizing as the current model. In some ways it actually lends itself more readily to the planned degree of customizing that can be achieved. Most modellers will have a toy fair or car boot sale nearby and, once you have mastered a few tricks and techniques, they can usually provide a relatively inexpensive source of buildings. As long as they are more or less intact, their overall condition is immaterial.

To keep this exercise remaining as close as possible to the work needed on a new kit, it is best to disassemble the 'ruin' into its component parts. On this version it required little more than gentle finger pressure and the occasional insertion of a scalpel blade to recreate its kit form. While doing this and studying what was left, the decision was taken on how to restyle the building radically. Eventually, since this was to be no more than a stand-alone project, I opted to show two contrasting styles on the one building. Half would be finished in a revised type of brickwork and the other would be wood-planked on a brick plinth. The canopy over the road entrance, together with the access doors, would remain the same; the internal loading dock would be wood floored but recessed to allow vehicles to reverse in; and finally the external office would be lowered to the more prototypical ground-level position.

Having disassembled the shed the following sequence, viewed from the roadside, was undertaken: the rear wall and right-hand gable would be brick, while the front wall, left-hand gable and office would be timber clad; the roofs would remain slate.

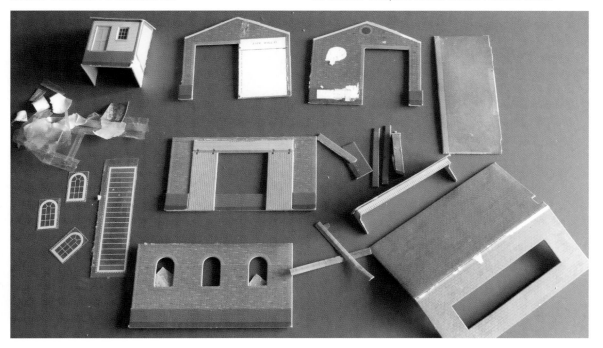

The bits left over after taking apart a rather battered second-hand model are not very impressive, but they are the starting point for the coming challenge.

PREPARATIONS

There are a few tasks to be done before the actual modelling can commence.

Paint all interior walls and the roof underside with white emulsion. Select suitable new windows from any available glazing sheets. Select brick and tile papers as required and suitable plain paper for the planked areas. Select balsa and hardwood strip for dock, doorway, inner walls and roof trusses. The brickwork at the base of the external office should be trimmed off with a scalpel.

EXTERIOR/MAIN WALLS (BRICK FINISH)

Reassemble the rear wall and the right hand gable. Check that it is square and add ¼in reinforcing strip on the inside to maintain its position as square and vertical.

Using ordinary paper glue, cover the whole length of the plinth, including turning inwards around the entrance. Lightly score the back of the chosen paper

on each corner to ensure a clean and sharp 'bend-back' and fix in place.

Repeat the same exercise for the main walls, making sure there are no air bubbles, the corners are sharp corners, and that the sheet is securely glued all around the windows and entrances.

Allow adequate time for it to dry, then carefully cut each window area corner-to-corner in an 'X' shape below the arched top. Bend the three triangular shapes (sides and bottom of the window aperture). Secure the flaps by gluing them neatly to the edges inside and cut off the surplus. Repeat this stage around the entrance.

The tops of the arches need several smaller cuts all around to enable the brick paper to follow the curve. Treat as above: glue, bend inwards, smooth down and trim the excess.

Touch up the overlapping brick paper on the interior walls with white enamels or emulsion.

The original finish had a pleasing effect of contrasting quoins and decorative brickwork to the

The gable end shows the additional decorative quoins, but reveals all too clearly the white paper edges that will definitely need the attention from pastels or paintbrush.

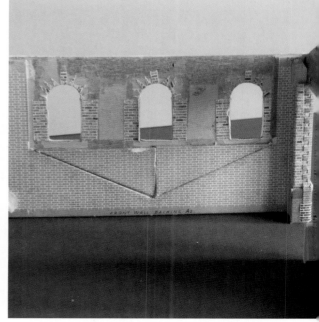

This interior shot shows how the brickwork has been turned in to mask the edges of the window apertures and around the doorway. The wall is now ready for the new glazing. It still looks untidy, but there's more work yet to be done.

These are the outer walls selected for the brick finish. This version has a more yellowish tone, set off by the darker colour of the decorative elements. As usual engineer's blue bricks are used on the plinth.

windows and doorway. These can be reproduced from the same style sheet used for the plinth. This is not a quick task and needs a sharp scalpel, good light, a steady hand and considerable concentration. Each side of the quoins should be alternate 'whole brick/half brick'. The required strips of two bricks wide are cut vertically from the sheet. Working from two whole bricks immediately above the plinth, nick the sheet and remove the next and each alternate half brick from the strip. In total you will need two 55mm lengths for the quoins and two 45mm lengths for the doorway (a total of 200mm). Once you have made the cuts and separated the items, lightly score the vertical centre lines down the reverse. Bend them fully over and then re-straighten, brush them with paper glue and fix in place, ensuring crisp corners by pressing down with the back of a scalpel blade.

From the sheet, cut suitable pre-printed arches and vertical bricks for the door lintel and window-sills. Glue them in place. Cut a single small strip of horizontal brickwork to run between the bases of the arches and extend all round both walls to replicate the decoration.

This exercise has effectively obscured the pre-printed round window on the gable end, an attractive feature that it is notoriously difficult to replicate. Trying to cut an accurate 8mm diameter hole in stiff card is not for the faint hearted. I have found, however, that the W11 and W12 factory window sheets from Truetexture contain not only the main arched versions but also similarly styled small round versions in black and white, respectively. This was simply stuck down on top of a black painted panel and the matching arch and sill duly added.

Fix the selected new windows, adding extra depth to the frames with thin strips from self-adhesive labels. Glue in place an impact adhesive. The roof glazing also needs some slivers of self-adhesive labels to break up the run of glazing bars. These should be added over the planned location(s) for the roof trusses.

EXTERIOR/MAIN WALLS (PLANKED FINISH)

This pair of walls, which include the vehicle access doors, is a more challenging part of the project. As well as a rail entrance, they also incorporate the small goods office at the gable end. We therefore have to consider the position of doorways and windows, and there are few opportunities to use full-length planks.

The first step is to assemble our stockpile of planks. The choice of paper (rather than card) should not be less than good quality writing or copy paper (80gsm) while low quality drawing paper (150gsm) is as thick as one should go. In the real world these planks would be around 1ft deep (4mm to scale) and that is a fairly easy measurement with which to work. They can be quickly produced in long strips with a simple cheap paper cutter. This is a useful tool especially if you intend to move into agricultural and small industrial structures, which require many planks. A steel rule and scalpel, though, will do the job just as well. Remember that the longer the strips you attempt to cut the greater the risk of error. I suggest a maximum of 5in (125mm) is more than enough and will fit comfortably within your six-inch steel ruler. On the model the fitted planks should be around 8ft

(32mm to scale) in length, but this can be suggested quite simply when painting. Each successive plank will overlap the previous one, so make sure you cut enough for the whole job.

Continue the plinth brickwork around the base of the wall. If you wish you can extend it around the office, but I have found that it looked better and more realistic to stop at the end of the main wall. When laying the planks it is desirable to make them appear to continue behind the large sliding doors, gently easing these away from the structure with the point of the scalpel.

Cut your first batch of strips into roughly 25mm lengths ready to fix to the shorter right-hand section of the wall. Brush a thin layer of paper glue onto the first plank and, with one end tucked neatly under the door, fix it immediately above the brick plinth.

Continue up the wall, overlapping each successive layer (twenty in all) to reach the eaves. The planks will slightly overhang the corner of the wall. Allow the glue to dry and trim off the excess.

Moving now to the left-hand end, it is best to lay the planks at the base of the office. Five or six should be sufficient to bring them to the same level as the top of the plinth. From here upwards you can start

Some preparatory work needs to be done on the pair of planked walls. Lots of planks are needed, so you should assemble a good supply of your chosen paper, a large set square or rolling ruler, and a sharp H pencil.

First mark out the depth of each plank down one side of your paper. It is not necessary to be absolutely accurate, but it should be as close to 4mm (scale 1ft) as you can manage.

Carefully align your set square with the edge of the paper and work down the sheet, drawing the horizontals from each dot.

Using a paper-cutter will definitely speed up the exercise, but you should take care to keep it correctly aligned and cut the longest planks that you can.

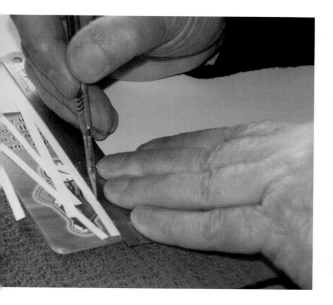

There are a couple of tips to pass on if you are using a scalpel. Make sure your blade has a keen edge and that the tool is as level as you can make it, maximizing its cutting power rather than just employing the point. A strip of masking tape on the underside helps prevent the steel rule from slipping.

Applying the planks to the road side of the shed. You will notice some have already been positioned as this is more easily done while two portions are separate, although this is not essential.

the planks just beneath the sliding doors, as before, extending them right across the remainder of the office wall. You will need a few shorter ones for the section that is higher than the office roof. Once again allow the glue to dry and trim off the excess.

Turning the corner, we are now faced with the front wall of the office with its doorway and a small window, both of which should still be holes at this stage. To keep things tidy, start by carefully positioning to each plank so that there is an accurate join with those on the already finished wall. Run the strips right across the face the structure. As always you should make sure that they are securely glued around the doorway and window.

While waiting for this section to dry, you can turn your attention to the gable end of the shed itself. This can be a bit tricky. The easiest approach is to start by planking it all across the entrance. Run the strips from the office and glue them to the small section of the buttress or outer wall. Continue up until you are level with the top of the office roof. You can then apply all the remaining strips across the full width of the gable end until you reach the apex or ridge.

The glue on the front of the office should now be dry and you can trim away the excess ends. You now need to carefully cut out the door and window aper-

tures. This is made easier if you can hold the assembly so that light can shine through the interior of the office. This will help you to see more clearly the outlines where you need to cut. This is another job for which a truly sharp scalpel will pay dividends. Simply prick through the paper planks and make sure the resulting cuts are absolutely tight to the edges of the door and window frames. (This stage will demonstrate why secure fixing and well-dried glue are essential.)

Reglaze the window and refit the door using a universal glue. Touch up the frames and the edges with acrylics or enamels to suit.

These procedures should by now have allowed the planks on the gable end to dry sufficiently for you to trim off the excess and cut away the rail entrance with a scalpel in the same way as the office door and window.

The rail entrance is sufficiently wide for you to be able to model the timber frame uprights required to support the necessary and freshly made doors. The construction method is the same as that employed for the Superquick goods shed, but for this kit they should be 20 × 55mm. The uprights can be made from balsa or hardwood strip at least 2mm square (6in to scale) and cut to fit. Use PVA or universal glue to hold them in place.

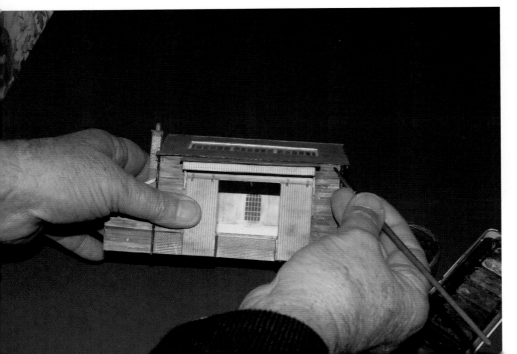

Painting the planks with watercolours can be done at any stage once everything is properly fixed, dried and trimmed. Work fairly quickly with a series of washes from a palette of white, through various shades grey to black. Use a reasonably sized brush, but also have an ultra-fine one handy to pick out the ends of the planks (roughly 8ft in length) or the odd nail-head.

The last remaining planking is for the left-hand or rail side of the office. The procedures are the same as before, but working from the main wall out. Trim when ready and then paint all the planks with your watercolours, using an assortment of pale greys through to almost black.

THE ROOFS

We can now turn our attention to the roofs, starting with the office. I chose to finish my version with an asbestos cladding as if the structure had been repaired at some point. It is best to cut a new roof template from your mounting board (40 x 50mm in this instance) and secure this in place using PVA with the appropriate overhang at the eaves. Using simple paper glue, add the cladding or tile paper and trim to fit. Finally add barge-boards from thin card and a strip of very thin paper to represent the protective lead flashing where the roof meets the gable end. Roll-your-own cigarette papers are ideal for this job.

We now need to add or replace the chimney, which must now be positioned in the far right-hand corner of the roof. My version was battered and broken, but it was straightened by inserting a section of $1/4$in balsa. New and matching brick paper was used to re-cover it and the appropriate capping strips and pot were duly added. Apply more lead flashing where the stack meets the roof.

At this point the main roof should not have been fixed permanently. On my model I replaced the glazed section with a piece from the spares box. This came from an old Superquick island platform and so had the inevitable yellow glazing bars. These and the frames where covered and given extra depth by using small strips of self-adhesive label and a quick touch of white drawing ink.

The roof itself, together with the canopy over the vehicle bay, was covered with tile paper. I chose to use Superquick grey, which I have always found to be useful, being neutral in colour and responding well to pastel weathering. Having added the ridge tiles and made up some barge-boards, this sub-assembly was again put to one side. On this model any significant roof details would be barely visible under normal operating conditions, so I chose not to include any, but if you wish to the procedures would be exactly the same as above.

The small canopy required little attention, although as usual I scribed the planking and shaved the visible edges to make them noticeably thinner and look less like cardboard.

INTERIOR LOADING DOCK

The necessary customization of the interior loading dock is the same irrespective of whether the main structure is to be built of brick, timber or even stone. It measures some 52mm wide (13ft to scale) and occupies the full length of the shed, making it a suitable subject within which to include a proper vehicle loading bay at the road entrance. This was a very common feature and allowed lorries to be handled almost completely under cover. It also permitted some side-loading as well as via the tailgate.

I opted to make the recess or bay 20mm deep (5ft to scale) and across the full width of the doorway. A further small recess was also cut into the original card base to permit the inclusion of some access steps from ground level to the dock. (This feature is all too often overlooked, implying that the goods porter must somehow manage to scramble several feet up onto the dock.)

Once these had been cut out, the original card platform was then planked with $3/16$ x $1/32$in balsa strip (5 x 1mm) and given a quick brush with a mix of greyish/white watercolours. Note that, unlike hardwood, plain watercolour is quite sufficient for balsa and needs no primer.

The dock was then reassembled using the original front supporting wall (rail side) and fabricating the new support walls around the loading bay from suitable thick card. All the walls where then covered in the same brick paper used for the plinth. The steps were made from balsa strip and, together with the whole subassembly, were duly fixed with PVA.

INTERIOR (PLANKED VERSION)

We can now turn our attention to modelling the interior woodwork of a timber-built structure. In most cases the framing will rarely be seen, but it's pleasing to know it's there just in case. In this instance we can start from platform level up. (If dealing with a planked rail-side wall it would be plinth level up.)

Offer up and mark with a pencil where the top of the platform will be. Select your chosen balsa or hardwood square strip: the main posts can be around 2mm (6in to scale) and the bracing struts can be somewhat less.

This is only supposed to give an impression of the interior and not be an architectural exercise in miniature. It is not necessary to be strictly accurate, but it is worth drawing a few designs on a scrap pad until you get something that looks about right. Then transfer that design with pencil to the actual interior walls. Before you tackle the framing, it is usually sufficient to draw the outer planks as horizontals 4mm apart using a hard pencil, or lightly scribe them with a scalpel point or needle tool. Try it on any small

section that might be less frequently seen and judge for yourself whether it's worthwhile.

Start by gluing the base horizontal timber with PVA all the way round the gable and side wall, using the pencil mark as the datum line. Let the one on the side wall run the whole length and fix the gable end portion 2mm in from the edge to ensure a snug fit. Add the uprights from the 2mm square, cut to 2mm short of the top of the side wall, and then fix the top horizontal above them. The main rectangular frames are now complete, and the diagonals and cross members can be cut and glued into place according to your drawing. Once done, give them the same whitewash finish with emulsion to blend them in.

The inside loading dock has been reclad with balsa wood planks. Access to the shed for road vehicles has been improved by providing a lorry bay. There is a recess for a small flight of steps leading to the dock.

The interior walls are here seen marked with position lines for the timber skeleton. Tasks like this are better done before the general coat of whitewash is applied.

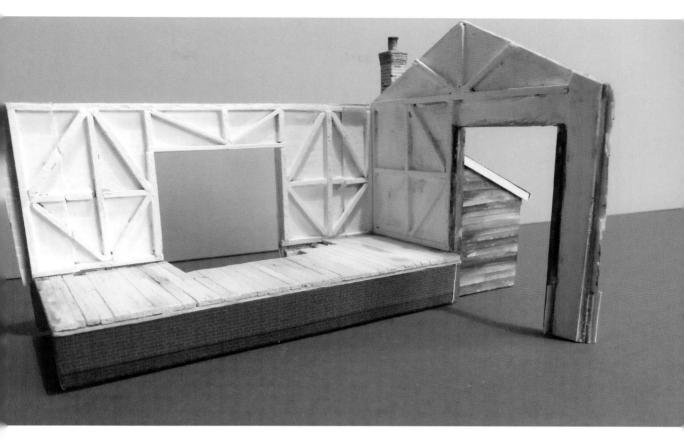

The main supporting timbers, made from balsa strip, have joined the relaid loading platform. Everything is now treated to reproduce the faded limewash and the generally dusty and warm atmosphere of a wooden shed.

REASSEMBLY

The time has now come to complete the assembly phase following exactly the same procedures as for any other kit. The fact that for this exercise I have used two contrasting styles makes no difference. The usual rules of 'square and vertical' apply with all types of kit and you should quickly have the basic box structure together. You may have deliberately omitted some of the tabs in the original kit, so it is particularly important to ensure that your corner joints are solid. Triangular fillets or 1/4in square strip balsa or hardwood sections can always be added as reinforcements at points that are likely to remain unseen. The final assembly can be completed once any additional internal detailing, such as loads and clutter, has been carried out. I did consider an inter-

nal crane-type hoist, but this seemed like overkill on a shed of such modest dimensions.

The last task is obviously the weathering of the structure as a whole. Once again this is a simple task of brushing on various suitable tones of pastel dust from your available palette.

The Superquick range, especially these earlier models, does not exactly offer the Rolls-Royces of the kit world. With a modicum of care, however, they make workmanlike and inexpensive structures for the beginner. If one exercises some imagination and effort, even the basic kit can be lifted to a higher and more realistic level. If they can be taken one stage further, then they form sound basic structures upon which to carry out most of the techniques used by the scratch builder.

ABOVE AND BELOW: *The brick finished wall and gable end have been lightly weathered and most of the visible paper edges disguised. The roof is definitely not the neatest and needs some extra attention. The glimpses of the internal woodwork are an attractive addition and the replacement glazing from Truescenes is a definite improvement. The new windows, though, did not fit until the bottom panes had been removed.*

After the paper planks have been trimmed to fit and the side/gable end glued into position, it is then possible to start painting – unless you have already done this. Whichever method you choose, the end product should look like this, a neat example of a rural goods shed. The subtle variations of tones and density of colour are typical characteristics of well-weathered timber.

The Prototype Watlington goods shed has a tile-strip roof, individually planked walls and a detailed interior. It has graced the author's layouts for more than forty years.

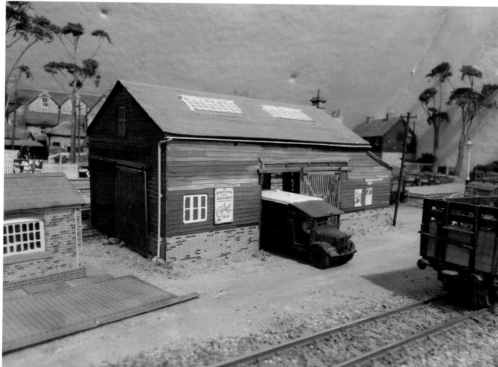

The current Superquick shed, albeit with additional details, is here seen in its temporary place on the author's branch terminus. It looks quite at home in this typical position.

The task of transforming the second-hand early version of the Superquick shed seemed a daunting prospect, but the finished result shows what can be done with a bit of effort. The finished model would make a perfectly acceptable substitute at Watlington.

BUILDING AND DETAILING THE METCALF SHED

The Metcalf goods shed, the second of our readily available off-the-shelf examples, is altogether different. It is larger, more realistic and far more complex and thorough in its design.

It would be laborious to set out the same step-by-step procedures as we did in the previous examples. This time I will assemble the shed with one side modelled as accurately as possible but remaining true to the manufacturer's instructions. The other side will be customized to see if it can be made to look as if it was built by a railway south of that hypothetical line from Birmingham to the Wash.

Metcalf has provided excellent assembly instructions and I wholeheartedly recommend that these are carefully studied with the kit laid out for easy reference. There are many individual parts and accurate assembly requires each to be positioned in the correct sequence. Indeed the instructions, on the printed sheets and on the frets themselves, are among the best I have encountered. They are the very epitome of clarity and are further enhanced with some sound general advice and helpful tips.

Since it costs about twice as much as the older Superquick kit, it should be no surprise that opening the packaging reveals more for your money. There are six A4 card frets of the kit itself, a further fret of plain card 'reinforcements and packing pieces' and eight A4 pages of fully illustrated instructions. The finished product includes a loading dock, offices and the invaluable bonus of a weighbridge or weigh house contributing to an overall footprint that is 70 per cent larger than the Superquick. It is also worth stressing the clean and accurate cuts to the frets themselves. Each item separates readily and very little scalpel work is required. The windows are well printed on substantial acetate - and have the correct white, rather than yellow, glazing bars.

The high-street alternative to Superquick is the more expensive one from Metcalf. The instructions are a model of clarity and, while not a speedy project, the finished item is robust, realistic and needs little or no extra input.

Metcalf has also included a larger degree of relief detail that, when combined with strengthening pieces and thicker acetate windows, delivers a very solid and robust end result.

Readers could be forgiven for thinking that such a kit might be beyond the skill levels of a new entrant to the field of card modelling. While it is not an easy model to throw together, its clever design and clear instructions place it firmly within the scope of the beginner. That said, it should not be rushed. My total build time, working on top of a bookcase measuring just 2ft by 9in, took about sixteen hours, including all the extra modifications and the final touching up process. Metcalf is to be congratulated on producing a kit that is a pleasure to assemble.

The end product will suit any reasonably sized goods yard. There are many similar prototype buildings located right across the country. Overlaying the different brickwork is an easy task and can help to give the structure an important local identity. This could be even further enhanced by repainting the existing green woodwork into the appropriate house colours of a particular company or British Railways

The Metcalf shed has here been built exactly to the instructions, apart from some work on the goods office. The printing process has delivered a commendably matt finish to some excellent artwork. Watercolours have been used to hide the exposed edges and light pastel dust has added some weathering, but otherwise the model is in 'as built' condition.

Despite the Metcalf kit's excellence, it is still a routine task to add some personalized touches. I would advise doing as much of this as you can before the assembly process starts. Experience and near-surgical skill with the scalpel, however, would make a retrofit exercise a real possibility, which could be very useful for anyone wanting to revamp an existing model. To prove the point, the new brick papers were applied to the finished model.

region, in which case the included doors will need extra care or even replacement.

None of its shortcomings are insurmountable or would deter me from recommending the kit. The main doors usually installed to secure the rail entrances, for example, are not included. The chimney stacks and some of the corners leave quite a lot of exposed card edges. Also the two plain brick halves of the rear wall of the weigh-house showed a marked variation in printed tone. A bonus, though, is that the kit includes a useful sheet of brick paper specifically for remedial or customizing work. I was able to put this to good use correcting these minor problems. The accompanying illustrations show these and the other tasks that were carried out.

In general this kit needs very little corrective work and is already well detailed. It would be possible to make the roof detachable, as in the previous example, but you need to decide if it is worth the effort. One side and a gable end were covered in a different brick finish, but an even more radical transformation could be achieved by using a suitable stone paper or even stone plasticard. I restricted any additional work to some simple pastel-weathering before installing the finished buildings on the wayside goods yard (see Chapter 4).

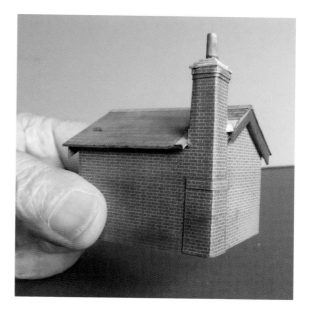

The weigh-house is a valuable addition to the kit, but it does need some attention using the brick paper supplied. The only minor criticism of the kit concerns the capping pieces for the chimney, which seem to be oversized and certainly don't look right when in place. I made a new top from the spare paper.

The small amounts of work that needed to be done to the main building were partly cosmetic as well as remedial: the chimney stack was improved and the steps benefited from some extra strips and engineer's blue bricks. The poor fit of the office was rectified using scrap card to extend the plinth around the office to help tie the two structures together.

RECENT DEVELOPMENTS AND FURTHER OPTIONS

To conclude this lengthy chapter on kit built goods sheds, it is only fair to take a look at some of the other products that are available. The market is expanding very quickly as a growing number of smaller companies and individuals take full advantage of the developments in computer technology. In some cases this may be limited to its use as a marketing tool, which offers them much greater flexibility than the traditional magazine advertisements.

Many of the new generation, however, are using it to the full as both a design facility and coupled with a delivery system straight to your desk via printed downloads. Several firms are also moving into laser-cut materials, including options to cut to the customer's own specifications. These latter are more advanced in concept and therefore are outside the scope of this book. They are intended for the more experienced modeller with more precise needs and, doubtless, with a deeper pocket to match.

This is in any case a tricky field to enter, since it poses awkward ethical questions for reviewers, authors and editors alike. On the one hand these new technologies certainly work to the advantage of the modeller. The products available are increasingly more accurate, of equal or higher quality, offer greater choice of prototypes, represent good value – and they certainly promote real modelling skills, which, it can be argued, is more than might be said for the ever increasing number off-the-shelf, ready-to-site structures.

There may be a downside, however, that will have a lasting effect. These new products effectively eliminate the retailer, from the traditional high street shop to the more specialist model railway emporium. The opportunity to browse through bits and pieces has always been a key factor to the retail sector. There has already been a decline in footfall as the demand for brass and white metal detailing items for rolling stock has been largely eliminated by the incredible advances in high-quality r-t-r stock. Nor will the regular monthly magazines remain untouched by these problems: the new breed of manufacturer/sup-

Freestone Models from Witney offer a comprehensive selection of current card-kits and accessories, together with their own versions of long-since vanished items. Their mail-order service is both prompt and helpful.

Scalescenes was among the first companies to enter the rapidly growing market for download kits and aids, offering a completely screen-orientated service, from the well-illustrated catalogue to the delivery of the kit to your terminal. The value and perceived quality of the range is outstanding. A kit of about 20 A4 pages costs less than £5 (as of early 2015) and this may be printed as many times as you wish. The artwork and general 'buildability' are both of the highest quality.

plier needs do little more than take sufficient space to remind readers of its existence and then simply direct them to its website.

This 'progress' must be accepted as the likely way forward. It is immaterial whether I like it or not: it is the future and doubtless there will be further progress before this little book is published. So make the most of this brave new world but don't abandon the old ways entirely. As modellers we will always want the very best in that best of all possible worlds: we need the high street and local dealerships, the magazines, auction houses, toy fairs, car boot sales and the internet too. Wherever you can, shop around within your budget and spend wisely to ensure that all these sources continue to flourish. Without local shops where would we go for that tube of polystyrene, pack of rail joiners, tin of

enamel, or even the odd wagon? These small items are not economic to buy online or by mail order. Local shops are friendly and helpful places: I for one am more than happy to buy my locomotives, kits and vehicles from mine.

The question remains how well these newer or regenerated products stack up in terms of their finished quality and their overall construction experience – or 'buildability' if you prefer? The answer, of course, is pretty well in every case. There are considerable differences in price and the amount of work and effort required, but they certainly command attention. Just like Superquick and Metcalf, they make acceptable additions to the layout as well as providing excellent training grounds towards scratch building. They are here to stay and will no doubt continue to grow in popularity to the point when they are almost commonplace.

CHAPTER FOUR

THE GOODS YARD

At this point we need to take a closer look at the goods yard in the chosen era. I imagine that very few readers will have had much experience of a goods yard during the 1950s. Even those of my generation who were spotters and enthusiasts probably never gave the yards a second glance. A broad overview will provide some guidance in achieving that railway-like appearance and enabling prototypical operations.

THE ROLE OF THE GOODS YARD

We have already established how vitally important the traffic in goods and merchandise was to the early railway builders. This importance, albeit increas-ingly diminished, would remain pretty constant until the end of the 1950s. Although road transport had certainly begun to capture some of the market immediately after the First World War, its impact was initially limited. There was a simple reason for this in that even pre-grouping companies and certainly the Big Four were quick to purchase their own vehi-cles and thus managed to stifle some of the possible threat from local carriers. In our chosen period the crimson and cream BR delivery vans and lorries were a common sight on rural roads and city streets, fulfill-ing exactly the sort of role envisaged by the railways' founders. The goods yard at each station had become a railhead for its surrounding area. Regular routes and times enabled road vehicles to deliver incoming

The goods yard in the days of steam was at the very heart of the local community. This was even more evident in the years immediately before and after the Second World War. Despite the obvious constraints on the individual during the decade of austerity, industry and commerce were working flat out to get the country back on its feet and rail traffic was at its zenith. STEAM MUSEUM OF THE GREAT WESTERN RAILWAY, SWINDON

merchandise from the railway more or less to the recipient's doorstep. Outgoing items would also be collected and returned to the station for onward transhipment. It was a very efficient service that would often see single items travelling the length of the country in twenty-four hours.

It was for the railways, however, a costly exercise since charges were controlled by the government and they remained 'common carriers', required by law to take any consignment offered to them. Fortunately such political constraints have no place on our layouts. We can just enjoy buying and positioning attractively coloured vehicles within our scenes.

Next to nothing remains of the once busy goods yards. Even those that still exist on our preserved railways, often with their goods sheds, are much altered in layout and use. The vast majority of yards proved to be potentially valuable building land and have now disappeared under industrial estates, housing developments and road improvement schemes. To get any true idea of their appearance in the 1950s will need another trawl through the photographic albums and even a study of 25 inch to the mile Ordnance Survey maps.

BASIC CONSIDERATIONS

There are, however, some basic principles that we can all follow despite the inevitable constraints of potential space or our existing track plans. Even though a goods yard can be anything from a short single siding for the local coal merchant to a complex of trackwork spread over an acre or more and serving an infinite variety of customers, these common principles will still apply.

- Goods yards were usually sprawling affairs built when land could be commandeered quite cheaply. More spacious yards will look more realistic.
- Space for road vehicles must appear generous. Remember it was intended for use by horses or traction engines drawing substantial four-wheeled wagons. Tight turning circles and three-point turns were not really an option. This space is needed around the goods shed and any other area where loading and unloading will take place.
- Railway companies preferred, but could not always manage, to keep goods facilities separate from passenger or public areas. Individual entrances are

Even the smaller rural goods yard would have a weighbridge and office, usually sited near the entrance to the site. AUSTIN ATTEWELL

End-docks, used by both military and civilian operators, were a convenient and simple answer to the transhipment of vehicles and wheeled machinery. AUSTIN ATTEWELL

quite common, along with the necessary additional fencing.

- Yards were laid out to reflect the traffic they were intended to carry. Those in or near population centres would have more space allocated for domestic and commercial coal deliveries, together with bigger goods sheds for general merchandise.

- Most decent-sized yards would have at least one crane capable of three to five ton lifts. These might be at ground level or sited on the loading dock. An additional hoist, sometimes even another crane, could also be found inside the goods shed itself.

- A weighbridge was a necessity; either adjacent to the goods shed or with a separate weigh-house near the yard entrance.

- A loading gauge is another essential. These would usually be encountered straddling the exit road from the yard but were sometimes attached to the outward doors of the shed.

- A separate siding or back road was useful for outgoing empties or for inward loaded wagons that could not yet be fitted into their eventual position.

- Where possible, the yard would be accessed via a goods loop clear of the running lines. Alternatively, a refuge siding and/or head shunt could be installed, accessed by a trailing-point. The likely level of operations at the yard would require it to be serviced by at least a twice-daily pick-up goods or 'fly'. Somewhere is needed to park the rest of the wagons, preferably clear of the running lines, while it shunts.

- In most cases yards were situated on just one side of the running line or lines. There are no fixed rules for this: it's often just a question of on which piece of land it was most convenient to build and subsequently to work.

- Some yards would have additional sidings installed. This often occurred during the Second World War to service new military installations nearby. Equally some may have had mini-branch lines and private sidings to service a quarry or mine. After these workings were exhausted, the facilities may have been left disused or torn up. These would provide the modeller with additional opportunities, perhaps a simple spur disappearing out of view and furnish-

There are a few rare instances where yard facilities are still operating forty years after their stations closed to freight traffic. The coal staithes at Corfe Castle look much the same as they did in the steam era, although more dilapidated.

ing extra in and out special traffic without much impact on the visual space within the layout.

- As a general rule, the more significant the volume of outgoing perishables or vulnerable traffic, then the more lavish would be the goods shed. Regular consignments of fruit and vegetables, textiles, footwear, agricultural produce, furniture and so on could all produce such a demand.

- The surfaces found in goods yards varied from well-laid cobblestones in the north to little more than packed earth and cinder in southern rural yards. It is often a complete mix with paved docks faced in engineer's blue bricks, approaches and vehicle areas surfaced with tarmac, and outer areas that turned, especially in winter, into mud and slush.

- Trackwork was usually ballasted, but often this was reclaimed spent ballast from the main line. The same was true of sleepers, especially on back roads or less busy yards. In some instances roadways and rails had to merge, in which case the 'four foot' would be built up to road level or inset into tarmac or cobbles, if you prefer.

- Vegetation was conspicuous by its absence, although rough grass, weeds, thistles and the ubiquitous pink Rosebay Willowherb could be found at the yard boundaries and around the buffer-stops.

- Yard lighting was uncommon since most facilities rarely operated after dark. In some cases electric light and hoist power were extended to the shed; it is the modeller's choice whether to include this. At bigger and busier yards there would certainly be a telephone line to the goods office and perhaps also to the often tumbledown shanties occupied by the coal merchants.

The associated track-plan diagrams (*see* opposite page) will show you some of the variations that can incorporate most of these features, which will also appear in model form in the special project build that follows.

MODELLING A GOODS YARD

There is one fundamental rule to be followed when planning the goods yard, irrespective of its size or complexity. If you wish to keep through services running at the same time as you are shunting the yard, you must have at least one loop and probably a head-shunt to keep the operations separate.

Watlington goods yard, the branch terminus on the author's 'Wessex Lines', is squeezed into a cramped corner space, but nonetheless the yard has all the main facilities. These include the shed, cattle dock, end dock, coal merchant's staithes and a back road. There is also a separate milk dock sandwiched between the carriage shed and the station platform. The whole occupies a triangular site barely 18 x 30in.

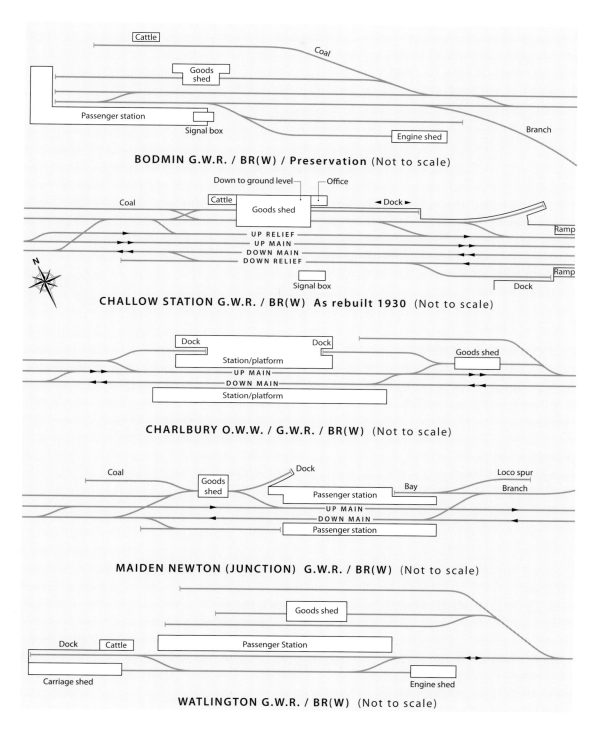

BODMIN G.W.R. / BR(W) / Preservation (Not to scale)

CHALLOW STATION G.W.R. / BR(W) As rebuilt 1930 (Not to scale)

CHARLBURY O.W.W. / G.W.R. / BR(W) (Not to scale)

MAIDEN NEWTON (JUNCTION) G.W.R. / BR(W) (Not to scale)

WATLINGTON G.W.R. / BR(W) (Not to scale)

Goods yards, even at relatively small stations, had to be laid out in a way that would meet the anticipated traffic within the constraints of the site itself. These random examples are just a few of the real-world solutions to the planner's problems. I can only speculate on the reasoning behind Challow's complicated design with its scissors crossover beyond the two-road goods shed.

This raises the question of available space and the need for careful planning of both the track and the wiring, especially if DC only. The single-track branch is always less of a problem since the terminus and any intermediate stations will be sure to have a loop where services can cross or be parked to allow other movements to take place.

This problem was as much a headache for the builders of the real railways as it is for the modeller. Each company had its own ideas on the best solution for each location. The accompanying diagrams show examples of these applied to both branches and secondary main lines. Given sufficient room on the modeller's layout, they could be reproduced exactly with total confidence in that they worked. With space at a premium, however, coupled with the need to use off-the-shelf point-work, some compression and simplification is probably inevitable.

KEY CONSIDERATIONS

As with most aspects of model railways, there must always be some compromise. In the case of goods yards it is necessary to balance at least the following key elements:

• Prototype track plans
• Space available on layout
• The requirement for continuous through running
• The availability of the required/desired point-work
• The frequency and scale of yard shunting
• The positioning of 'on-track scenic elements'
• The methods of uncoupling: auto or manual
• The method of point operation: mechanical, electric or by hand
• The background scenario for the yard's location and services.

The deciding factor of any project, however, is ultimately its cost.

While each of these elements has its own degree of importance the two most critical will inevitably be those of space and point-work, both of which are absolutes that cannot be changed. We all fall into the trap of drawing lines on a scrap pad or sheet of graph paper and then wondering why our elaborate track plan occupies three or four times as much space as intended. It is well worthwhile keeping a written record of exactly how much space is needed by each type of point and each basic piece of track geometry.

A pair of correctly aligned tracks, for example, should be 50mm apart centreline to centreline, or approximately 80 mm from outer sleeper to outer sleeper. That applies irrespective of whether the points we are using are set track or universal long radius. The set track and short radius points are 7in (about 180mm) long; 8½in (215mm) medium radius; 10in (250mm) long radius. A single crossover between two tracks therefore occupies 14¼in (360mm), 17¼in (440mm) and 20¼in (515mm), respectively. A ladder of, say, four parallel storage sidings from three points will be anywhere from about 27in (685mm) up to about 40in (1,000mm) when using the long radius type.

It is a stark choice between over-sharp radii or fewer sidings. Some space savings can be obtained by the judicious insertion of single or double slips, or the always useful three-way points. The latter, being medium radius, will achieve a ladder of four sidings within just 26in (660mm) and using only two points. The former, while allowing maximum operating flexibility, can nonetheless be geometrically confusing. At first glance the double-slip looks like a switchable long-crossing. Don't be fooled by the fact that, when it has to cross or join parallel straight tracks, it is not straight track but rather two medium radius curves, and these need to be curved back towards each other at the exits. I would always recommend testing this with Peco point templates. The single-slip, however, has the same geometry as a straight-track crossing and is that much easier to incorporate on the plan.

I have deliberately avoided the question of point operation. There are so many alternative methods that to select just one would be an implied criticism of all the others. The choice is yours.

PLANNING THE YARD

For the purpose of this particular exercise I have opted for an amalgam of two stations on the Oxford, Worcester and Wolverhampton Railway (sometimes known as the 'Old Worse 'n Worse').

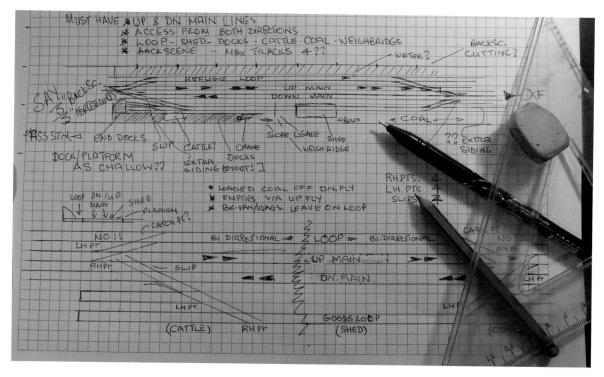

The following text appears within the planning sketch image:

MUST HAVE * UP & DN MAIN LINES
* ACCESS FROM BOTH DIRECTIONS
* LOOP - SHED - DOCKS - CATTLE - COAL - WEIGHBRIDGE
* BACK SCENE - MAX TRACKS 4??

Planning is nothing more technical than a series of sketches that take us from what we would like to what we can probably achieve. It includes the likely track-plan, where the key features might be located, the point-work required and a few notes on the probable operating procedures.

This is a double-track secondary main line with similar, but not identical, features to many of its wayside goods yards. Most of these were quite compact across the tracks but extended laterally to around 1,000ft (300m). To model them to scale would require a total length of 400cm or just over 13ft; add in sufficient room for the necessary curves to make it a part of a continuous layout and you need a layout at least 20ft (600cm) long. This would be a pretty ambitious goal for even the experienced solo modeller. Nonetheless, by the judicious use of a couple of slips, some compression and some extra point-work, we can design a personalized and real-istic version. It offers continuous running and more than enough potential work for even the busiest of pick-up goods services.

The yard itself, including the access point-work from the main line, requires some 78in (200cm) in length but a very modest width of just 18in (46cm), including some scenic background. Allowing a bit

more compression and the necessary curves at each end, which actually start with the crossovers on the main line, a continuous layout could be squeezed into a total length of less than 13ft (4m), a large but not unusual size for such a home-build project. The total width required would, of course, depend upon what one wished to do with the other three sides. The project, for convenience, is built on two A1 sheets of foam board linked by a sheet of A3. If space long-ways is available then the A3 could be usefully replaced by another A1 sheet.

The beauty of the Peco point templates is that they allow the modeller endless freedom to test and approve or eliminate plans before purchasing any points or track. Using the A2 scrap pad and half-size points, it is possible to come up with something that looks right and seems feasible. The full-size plan would verify most of this as well as disprov-ing another idea, the substitution of set-track curved points for the universal ones. It could be done but

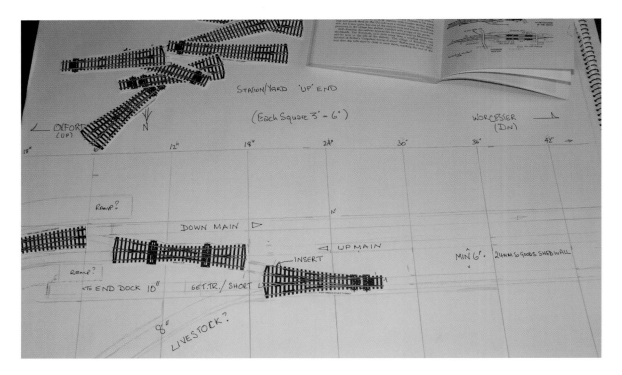

The initial planning stage with the A2 scrap pad marked on grid squares at a scale of 3in equals 6in and incorporating half-sized photocopies of Peco point plans. This will be the left-hand (station-end) module.

When the half-sized draft plans have been accepted they are transferred at full size to the A1 and A3 foamboard module. Full-size Peco plans are used here and a few vehicles and structures positioned to give some idea of the eventual appearance.

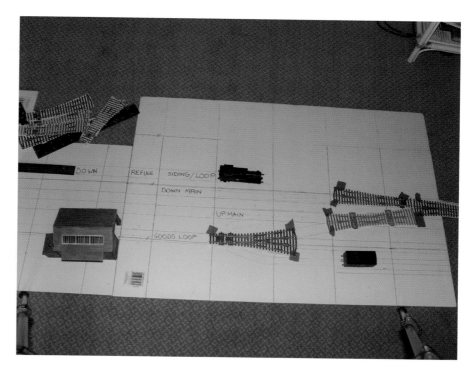

A closer view of the right-hand module, also showing the smaller A3 section. This added piece is needed to provide for the extra length to do justice to the Metcalf goods shed. The gap is mostly beyond the markings for the 18in wide working width and will be hidden by the back-scene.

it effectively widens the 'six foot' between the two running lines and pushes the down line too close to the outer wall of the shed. This is a useful and cost-free exercise.

The final layout included an extra loading dock for livestock, a separate siding for the coal yard, an extra holding siding for arrivals and dispatches and a prototypical setback or refuge loop off the up line. Both crossovers are correctly 'non-facing', but the goods shed loop, while entirely true to the prototype, is perhaps a little on the short side.

PREPARATION FOR THE PLATFORMS

Everything is now ready for the construction process to begin. In order to show the yard details step by step, I have chosen to construct it in modules, using my favoured medium of foamboard to create table-top sections. I will include the main lines and the refuge siding to illustrate the degree to which these are key elements of the plan. The track base will be playfoam and raised platform levels will be card. Everything employs exactly the same techniques as in any photographs of my finished layouts.

Having settled on the basic plan, the first step is to cover uniformly all the areas that carry the track-work and represent normal ground levels. The play foam can be stuck down with diluted PVA (half and half will suffice) or spray mount. Some of the sheets of this material are available in a self-adhesive version, albeit at roughly double the cost.

The sheets are laid intact but the approximate area of the platforms is not glued down: if necessary these could easily be cut away when the track plan has been re-marked. This is no more than a repeat of the test exercise and a suitable felt-tip pen is all that is needed to mark the outer edges of the points and tracks. In cases like this, where two or more modules are due for the same treatment, it is easier to make each mark across them all at the same time. When it comes to detailing them, they can still be handled consecutively.

With the track plan successfully redrawn, we can start track-laying. My preferred method is a fairly liberal coating of PVA, or even a No-More-Nails type of adhesive, evenly spread along the trackbed. It is essential that the track is firmly secured, since the later application of ballast glue

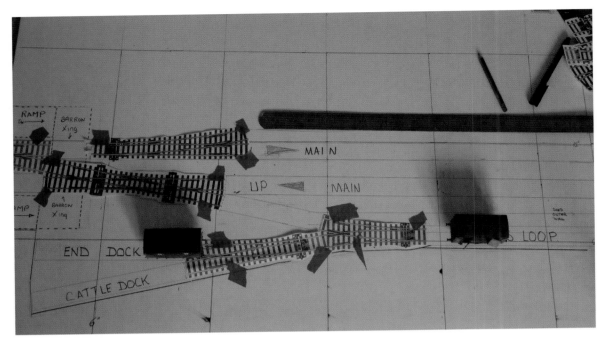

Close-up of the left-hand module.

may well cause it to lift. Most proprietary track systems have pre-drilled holes but they may be too large for one's chosen pins. I prefer to pre-drill mine using a 0.75mm bit in a pin vice. When laying more complex track sections, especially involving point-work, I prefer to fit the joining fishplates first and work away from the layout. This is particularly true with single or double slips where one has to juggle no fewer than eight individual rails and the requisite mix of insulated and non-insulated fish-plates. Once the joins are completed, simply press the items down onto the pre-glued trackbed and pin them in place. In the real world you would, of course, continue with this process right across the whole baseboard, but for this project I will cut mine at each module's edge.

PLATFORMS

Allow everything to dry and become firm, then trim off any unwanted play foam where the platforms will be. A good way of marking the platform edge is to take a longer wagon, like a bolster or bogie van, and hold a soft pencil or felt-tip pen vertically against the centre. Run this along the track to mark out the platform edges. Where you have a dock or bay plat-form you should mark both sides. By carefully cutting along the marks with a scalpel you should then be able to remove the unwanted sections. Don't throw them away, though, as some of the offcuts may come in handy later.

The next item on the agenda is to prepare the platform face, or support walls, and sufficient extra lengths to constitute the grid on which the eventual surface will sit. The height for these will be about 16mm above ground level to give the correct 12mm (scale 3ft) above rail height. You should check these measurements against your actual construction, just in case.

There could be a need for the platform edge to have a small overhang beyond the supporting wall, but this was not always the case on goods docks or platforms. Should you wish to include it, I suggest using a total overlap of no more than 3mm with the addition of a small strip, say two brick courses deep, of mounting board beneath. It's a question of whether you think it worth the effort, since most of it will not be seen from the normal viewing positions. If this option is taken up, the supporting wall must

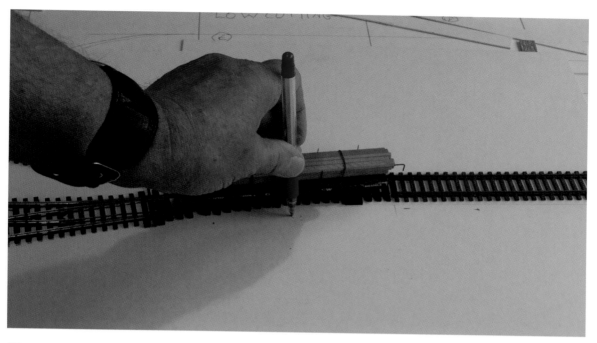

The platform/dock is largely straight, except for the area adjacent to the short 'Y' point serving the cattle pens and the end loading spur. This is the only place where there might be a problem with the overhang. In order to check for the necessary clearance a pencil or pen is used with a bolster-wagon chosen as having the longest wheelbase likely to traverse the curve.

eventually be positioned that same 3mm inside the drawn line.

We now need to cut out the actual platform top. There are two alternatives here. The first is to position a piece of the A2 sketch pad on the layout, secure it with masking tape, and then carefully trace the outlines of the running rails adjacent to the platforms. Remove the work and repeat the line the appropriate distance inside it to exactly replicate the platform edge line on the layout. This should be at least 25mm (1in) in from the track centreline. The alternative requires a similar exercise but using one or more sheets of tracing paper, which will enable you to reproduce the required line in a single operation.

Either way, it is now necessary to mark out the lines on the mounting board that will form the platform surface. Position the unwieldy A1 sheet so that the outer edges correspond with those of the baseboard and, using heavy scissors, roughly cut away the larger excess part to leave the more easily handled segment.

Overlay this workpiece with your drawing or tracing, again ensuring perfect alignment of the outer edges, then prick the line through onto the card. Join the dots and cut through with a scalpel or craft knife. Offer the finished piece up to the layout to double-check that all is correct and that the platform edge exactly matches the drawn lines.

Building the platform is a relatively simple task. Invert the workpiece so you can build on the underside. Offer up your prepared platform walls and supports and cut them to length to fit all the outsides. Cut a further batch to run transversely front to back at roughly 3in (80mm) intervals. Finally cut a last batch that will run along the work between the transverse supports, again at roughly 3in (80mm) intervals. That may sound complicated, but the photograph will show that isn't the case.

All this preparatory work should mean that everything is ready for the hot-glue gun. This gives a near-instant, rock-hard bond, but it does demand a speedy and precise operation. Fix the outer walls

The underside of the platform/dock with the supporting walls and bracings in place. The front wall has additional 'decorative' courses and is positioned fractionally inside the edge of the platform to give a small overhang. Front and back walls are fixed first and then pre-cut bracing strips, trimmed where necessary, are glued down with the cross members first to ensure the main walls remained vertical. Note the open well, which will accommodate the cattle pens.

first, making sure that all the corner joints are secure and all the supports are upright, and reinforcing with small sections of ¼in square balsa, if you wish. Next fix the longer transverse supports and ensure these are firmly glued to the outer walls. The final step is to drop in the short longitudinal strips, which must be a snug fit between the transverse members. The job is then complete. You may perhaps find that the glue is solid almost before you have had time to unplug the gun.

SURFACES

Attention can now be given to the actual surfaces, which in this case will be a fairly complex pattern of public access platforms and the various loading and unloading goods facilities. There are no fixed rules for any of this and it is very much a question of personal taste and the correct harmonization with any other station surfaces that may have already been completed. For this exercise I have chosen to include a variety of finishes in order to show what might be achieved. The basic assumption is that the public platforms have been, or will be, surfaced with simple Superquick grey paving. This has been extended to certain parts of the yard, but with cobble sets for the cattle dock and asphalt (emery paper) for outer sections. This latter surface would also extend beyond to the station car park and approaches.

The platform's outer walls will be brickwork with at least one section decoratively finished. It is worth noting that any cobbled areas will require that the platform edges replicate the usual finish of a row of hard-wearing engineer's blue brickwork.

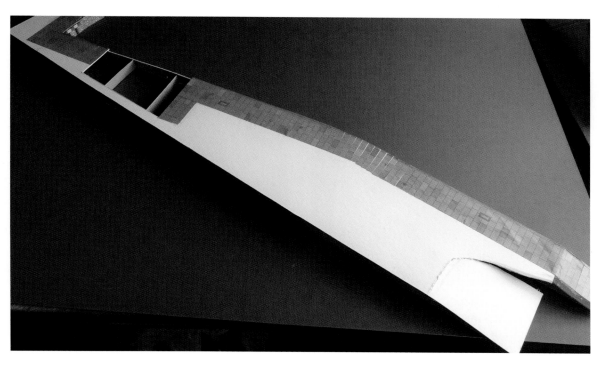

The paved section of the platform. The remainder will have a representation of an asphalt surface using fine-grade emery paper.

This view shows how the cattle dock will fit and the very simple design of the stop-blocks for the two end docks.

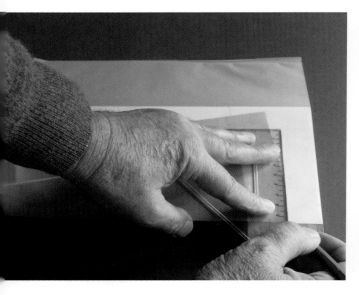

The emery paper has to be cut, like an oversize jigsaw, to fit around the paved areas. The easiest solution is to mark the required outline using tracing paper and a set square, holding the job steady with paperclips and bulldog clips.

Step two is to clip the tracing over the emery paper and, pressing heavily, transfer the outline to the surface and then cut it out with large, strong scissors. If the outline is sufficiently clear, double-check that two sheets are secure and properly aligned, cut through both pieces and then separate.

The black foam underlay has here been glued securely in place. At various times spray adhesive, dilute PVA, paper glue and even wallpaper adhesive have all been found to be quite satisfactory. Whenever there is relatively complex or critical point-work to be laid, it helps to try assembling it off the layout. This makes it much easier to position and connect all the many fishplates, rails and joiners, while still enjoying a little flexibility within the overall assembly. After test rolling a few wagons, the components receive a few smears of PVA or No More Nails and then pinned down.

All of the papered surfaces can be stuck down with paper glue, diluted PVA or spray adhesive. Whichever you choose, make sure that there is enough glue, but not too much; check that there are no air bubbles, stretches or rips, and that the edges are firmly fixed. Emery paper is slightly more tricky, since it has a propensity to curl up at the edges. Always try to minimize any joints; it is better to select an oversized sheet and sacrifice the waste rather than attempt to butt-join smaller sheets. Be more liberal with the glue and weigh down the whole area, perhaps with a pile of magazines.

After everything is fully dried, allow at least twenty-four hours before doing any necessary trimming and folding over the papers at the platform edge to cover the exposed edges of the mounting board.

Detailing is fairly minimal and need be little more than adding a kit-built platform crane, making up some suitable buffer stops for the end docks and building the cattle pens. The excellent plastic kit by Ratio could be used for the last of these, but it is not particularly easy to adapt. It requires a predetermined space, whereas cattle docks were generally constructed to meet the demand and fit in the space available. This will be the case on the project layout, which therefore needs a scratch-built installation.

ADDING THE CATTLE DOCK

On the real railways there were thousands of cattle docks, ranging from busy yards with perhaps three, four or more pens to simple single pens at a smaller station. They also varied in construction to an equal degree, from simple timber-built structures, old rails, concrete and steel tube, right through to all-welded steel angle and tube. For the project I chose to model the latter with two pens using a mix of plastic rod and small section 'L' and 'I' girders, augmented by spare gates left over from a previous job.

The pens can be built up directly on the platform itself. If this is too unwieldy for your workbench, measure up the footprint and cut out a sub-base from mounting board. Make it slightly oversize so it can be chamfered down to better merge with the main platform. Mark out the positions for the fences and gates. Cut the 'L' girders with a 2.5mm cross-section for the corners and 2mm gate posts into the required 24mm lengths. Cut the intermediates from 'I' girders into 20mm lengths. The rails need to appear quite robust yet remain small enough in diameter to enable the uprights to be drilled without weakening them. The recommended compromise is 1mm diameter (3 scale inches). Four rails equally spaced should be sufficient

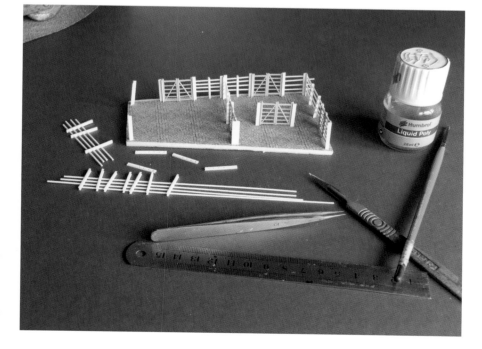

The scratch-built cattle dock under construction. The base is a laminate of the centres of two polystyrene picnic plates. The cobbles are from the ID range. The post and rail sections are from Greenscenes: the longer pieces are awaiting fitting.

The cattle dock nearing completion, showing the excess rails ready to be cut off with sharp, fine-pointed scissors.

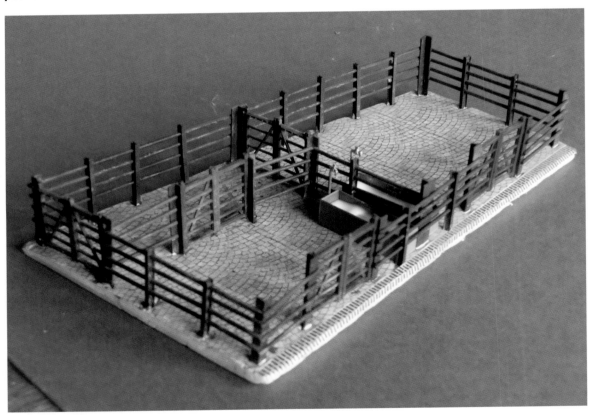

The finished cattle dock. This structure was built to fit and was completed in about sixteen hours from the first measurements. The ironwork was finished in matt black enamel before being weathered with rust-coloured pastel dust. Note the two water troughs knocked up from scrap plasticard with spare taps from the bits box. The model with two pens is of a size typical of most wayside or branch facilities. The method and materials can be used for any size or shape of dock.

and all the 'I' girders can then be drilled at suitable intervals. The 'L' girders do not need drilling as the rails will be 'welded' to their inner faces.

Once all the components have been prepared, return to the workpiece and mark out the locations for all the corner and gateposts and the uprights. Make all the necessary holes in the card using a bradawl or a small sharp screwdriver and plant the 'L' girders, securing them with universal or impact adhesive. Make sure they are vertical and face the correct way.

Trim the 1mm rod (rails) to approximate lengths to fit between the various corner and gateposts. Thread each set of four onto the planned number of 'I' uprights, but do not glue them at this stage. Plant the uprights, working one section at a time, and secure with universal or impact glue. The four rods (rails) can now be slid into their correct positions and poly-glued to the inner face of the left-hand 'L' corner post. Using sharp, fine-pointed scissors, cut off any excess from the right-hand end and poly-glue

in place. Double-check that everything is upright, horizontal and square, then apply a dab of liquid poly to secure all the rods to the uprights. Simply repeat the tasks until all the fences are complete.

You can now fix the gates in their open or closed positions, depending upon whether the pens will be occupied/empty (closed) or being used to load/ unload cattle (open).

Paint with enamels or acrylics to suit. If the pen has recently been maintained a probable finish would be matt black with matt white for the top rail and the top of each post. As with most ironwork, however, it is more likely to be a mix of very dull black and brown.

The two buffer stops at the ends of the docks could be pretty rough and ready. A frequently used method comprised a pair of partially buried rail sections as uprights with a sleeper bolted across them at wagon-buffer height. If you are using flexible track, these uprights can easily be cut from a scrap length. The sleepers can come from the same

A Beetle prize animal wagon provides visual reassurance for clearances.

It is always sound practice to offer up any workpiece as it is easy to make an error of a few millimetres when drawing and plotting. You might then add another couple when you transfer from one workpiece to another or when cutting out. Here the basic point-work has been positioned on the module without any problems. Most of the track used here has been recycled, an obvious saving when redesigning a layout.

source, but remember to trim off the moulded chairs. Alternatively a suitable sleeper-sized length of balsa strip will do the job. Glue with universal, rust enamel the rail sections and give the sleeper a coat of weathered black, with maybe a couple of white strips, suitably battered, where the buffers would impact. For the end dock a few tarred planks can be left nearby, ready for loading or unloading.

BALLASTING AND WEATHERING

Now that all the components are ready to be placed as required, we can turn to the major tasks of ballasting and weathering. Ballasting is simply the use of suitable granite chippings spread on loosely and secured with diluted PVA applied with a syringe or eye-dropper. There are countless variations and claims for 'best practice': misting the ballast with water and a drop of washing-up liquid via a garden spray; pre-painting and weathering the rails and sleepers before ballasting; disagreement over whether or not to carefully smooth the ballast before gluing or vacuum up the excess; rival claims about how much to dilute the PVA and so on. Here, though, is the traditional method I have used for laying about 400 yards of track over the years:

- Select the colour of ballast appropriate to the layout as a whole and in the finest size grain available, which is usually sold as 'fine' or 'n' gauge.
- For use within the yards I like to mix this with sieved garden soil, ash or sand: indeed anything that makes it look old and worn. For the public and vehicle areas I use a coarser mix, which is subsequently coated with a slurry of ready mixed filler and dilute PVA, toned to suit with emulsion paints or enamels.
- Apply the ballast liberally, but taking care to remove grains from the moving parts of point-work, and smooth it out with a small soft-point watercolour brush and a finger-tip.

- Fill it to sleeper height, since this helps disguise the out-of-scale trackwork.
- Mix the PVA, water and a drop or two of washing-up liquid in a small medicine bottle or similar container. I prefer a weak mix of around one part PVA to three parts water, as this flows more readily and is easier to apply with an eye-dropper.
- Where possible I like to do the whole job in one hit and then leave it alone for at least twenty-four hours in normal room conditions.
- It is inevitable that the ballast will migrate onto the tops of the sleepers, especially around the

A small soft watercolour paintbrush is a handy tool for getting excess ballast off the sleepers and smoothing things out prior to fixing with adhesive from an eye dropper.

The ballaster's toolkit. Display type lids from die-cast models make excellent containers for the various ballasts and for liquids. The white liquid is Astonish wood floor polish, which comes in 750ml bottles and often costs less than £1.00. The small palette knife is used to shovel smaller precise quantities of loose ballast and, as the glued covering dries out, to tamp it down and remove some of the excess. The bigger version is used to tamp down larger areas like the six foot or the general parts of the yards. Ballasting is not a quick exercise; it repays care and patience since the trackwork is in constant view and sloppy workmanship detracts from an otherwise quality model.

When cleaning the trackwork it is useful to have containers of adhesive and ballast close to hand. You are bound to discover holes or other features that require patching, as well as loose sections that require refixing.

chairs, so creating gaps under the rails. Remove the ballast on the sleepers with a small screwdriver or similar tool, and carefully fill the gaps with small quantities of ballast on the tip of a palette knife.

• Brush away any excess and reglue as required.

• Once everything is dry and suitably clear of unwanted bits, paint the rails and chairs with a scruffy reject watercolour brush. If you can find it I would favour the old Humbrol Track Colour. A suitable alternative would be a 'dark brown rust' or the various offerings from Precision or Rail Match. I'm happy to let the paint spread onto the sleepers around the chairs, since rust and wheel dust invariably discoloured these areas.

• If everything has gone to plan the black plastic sleepers will have become dull and dusty during the initial ballast spreading and should need no further attention. Several paint finishes are available, variously described as 'weathered sleepers' or 'sleeper grime', but I find that these tend to over-emphasize the sleepers rather than disguise them.

• When you are happy that there are no more holes and definitely no shiny bits of rail showing, it's then a simple task to clean off the tops of the rails with a track rubber.

• Make sure you double-check that your point-work functions properly and that no errant bits of ballast or paintwork impede either movement or current flow.

I should stress that this is simply my personal method and you may well find one of the many alternatives more suitable for your own project. The model press, especially Model Railway Journal, has recently advocated using Wood Floor Polish by Astonish as a substitute for the diluted PVA adhesive. This is not always easy to source, but is relatively cheap and may be found for less than £1. I have used both methods on the project boards with equal success.

There are as many ways to paint trackwork as there are modellers, especially with the wide availability of special colours and textures, airbrushes and aerosols. My own primitive method is limited to applying simple enamels with worn-out watercolour brushes. This project used Precision Track Colour, although I find it too bright. For contrast I've also shown the Railmatch offering. My choice, when it can be found, was for the duller, darker tones of the old Humbrol Track Colour; it may be worth examining the current Humbrol range for a close match.

The dust bowl. Simply rub the pastel gently along the emery board above a suitable tray or container. This small lid has room for small piles of different colours. They can be blended or used separately and are appropriate for buildings, landscape, rolling stock and even figures.

Apply using a fairly soft watercolour brush, either round, as here, or a smallish flat one, perhaps ¼in. Apply little and often, allowing the brush to collect just enough to cover an inch or so at a time.

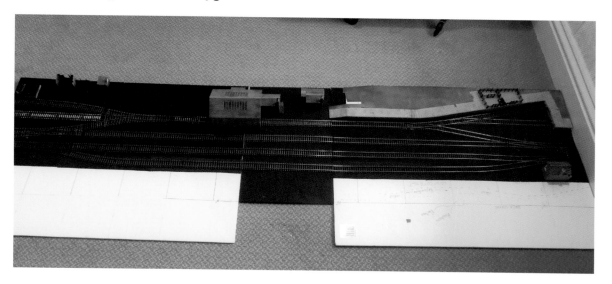

All three goods yard modules butted together. The black playfoam underlay covers the whole modelled area. When used in a purely main-line or through-road location, however, it would only form the trackbed. Modellers who are stuck for space will note that this form of longitudinal yard can easily be accommodated on the traditional 18in wide shunting plank, even with the 'down' lay-by loop and the 'up' and 'down' main lines.

The left-hand end of the module (the north or 'down' end in relation to the prototype) shows the complex trackwork that gives access to both the yard and the 'down' refuge loop.

The right-hand end, showing similar access from the south.

BRINGING IT TO LIFE

Once the ballasting is complete and tested for running, the platform module can then be secured in place with any of the adhesives already mentioned. Pastels should be used to weather all the various surfaces to help blend them together into a more uniform whole. Once done, we can add the various bits of permanent or removable detail.

The permanent features could include a suitable crane of up to about three tons capacity. This can be placed either at true ground level or on the raised platforms. A weighbridge and weigh-house are essential, as is the loading gauge. Other items should include the coal staithes (or heaps) and possibly the office or offices for the local merchants. Many rural yards also had additional storage sheds for the various contractors. The Ratio provender store makes a good kit-built example, while the scratch builder may prefer to make up a similar building of corrugated iron construction. These can be privately owned or company owned and rented out. They would be used to hold corn, fertilizers, feed or seed stuffs arriving or being dispatched in bulk to or from the railway en route from the individual farms.

Aerial view of the complete yard, the through lines and refuge loop. There is even room for a scenic backdrop that fits just within the 18in width allotted to it.

This view gives some idea of the amount of stock that might be accommodated in the yard or passing by.

ABOVE AND BELOW: *A reminder of how things used to be may be found on preserved railways. It would be unwise, however, to use these pristine examples as prototypes for our 1950s layout. Their immaculate condition would last barely a day in the hurly-burly of the smoky steam era.*

ABOVE AND BELOW: *While it is still possible to pick up second-hand wagons with opening doors, the easier option is to do it yourself. The donor wagons shown here were all acquired at local car boot sales for less than £2 each. It was then simply a question of some careful carving with the craft knife or scalpel, repainting, re-lettering and weathering, and the inclusion of the appropriate loads.*

The choice of removable features, which can actually be almost permanent, provided they do not impede operations, should be guided by the choice of the yard's location and customer profiles.

The yard crane chosen for the project is a straight-forward build of the Ratio kit. Colour schemes for the cranes varied, but black or dark grey are both safe options. The wagons and vans intended only as scenic accessories can easily be found at toy fairs or car boot sales for a pound or two. They will be non-runners, so the quality of their existing wheel-sets is unimportant, but some essential surgery will be needed.

Remember to paint the interiors as well as the exteriors and get rid of the proprietary couplings. The doors should then be carefully removed on what will be the platform side. This may entail removing the bodies from the underframes, and certainly removing the roofs on the vans. It is a laborious job, but repeat scoring down the edges, top and bottom is the only real answer. Be prepared to use a heavier craft knife as well as your scalpel and expect to use up more than one blade before the doors can be successfully separated. Replace them in their appropriate open positions secured with universal glue, which gives a little flexibility in respect of their final position. Add the loads or part loads, together with any porters or civilians engaged in the operations.

Cattle can be in the dock or being off-loaded from the farmer's vehicle. The coal merchant can be loading his lorry or unloading a wagon. Various Company, British Railways or British Road Services lorries could be seen, as could private vehicles from the farms or small businesses. In the early 1950s many of the latter would be either decrepit pre-war examples or ex-military trucks. The end dock could well have a new item of agricultural machinery await-ing collection on a Lowmac wagon, or an expensive car ready to be loaded into a waiting MOGO/DAMO or CCT. Along the platform edges one could position various open wagons or vans with doors open to show loading or unloading in progress.

Repaint the wagons in the liveries of your choice and do not forget to treat the interiors, since these will now be all too visible. As they are to be static exhibits, there is no need to replace their antique wheel sets. These conversions are simple enough to enable two or three vehicles to be done in an evening.

A new Fordson tractor has been delivered from the supplier and reloaded onto a BRS flatbed. The John Deare still on the bolster will be collected by the 'fly' for a later drop.

A few cows have been delivered by the local farmer, who is about to depart with his workers perched precariously on the kit-built Fordson Major. A 50p car-boot toy trailer and 50p Land Rover complete the scene. You may also glimpse the porters having a break.

All of this activity is down to nothing more exacting than using a bit of imagination, having a realistic back story, and the space and the budget needed to create each cameo. If this doesn't appeal, the yard can be deserted and the model fixed permanently at Sunday afternoon.

Cement bags being offloaded from a fitted van. The flatbed is another Base Toys product and the sacks are handmade from plasticine.

The yard crane is not needed here while more sacks are being offloaded from a drop-door open. Note the yard gate's notices and the sheeted-opens in the background.

The post-war building boom was still well under way in the 1950s. Wagonloads of cement, sand, tiles, timbers and 'fittings' were all regularly delivered to most wayside stations. Bulk sand is here being guided onto the Metcalf weighbridge to be checked. A Base Toys BRS lorry and Mike's Models figure complete this typical scene.

The ubiquitous Scammel Mechanical Horse is being loaded from the Metcalf shed. The vehicle is the Airfix/Dapol plastic kit version and the load comes from the bits box.

Sand is still being offloaded. This ground-level operation would be the norm for these bulk loads. The open wagon's drop door is at a convenient height for the road vehicles, and it was common to ignore the railway's reminders that such doors should not be used as shovelling platforms.

One of the local coal merchants has used the same technique and filled these sacks for his domestic round direct from the wagon. He takes a breather and strokes one of the many station cats. The pre-war flat-bed lorry is a white metal kit.

Further up the yard there is a more formal, but not necessarily common, coal staithe for offloading and storage. The lorry is a converted ex-Army Bedford QL; originally the tanker from the old Airfix refuelling set. In the background a handful of empty wagons await the returning 'up-fly'.

The coal yard as it might look later in our period, with JCBs doing some of the donkey work.

THE SCENIC SETTING

Most modellers probably choose to place the goods yard close to the operator's position, as featured on our modules. The background may well be more of a railway scene and effectively 'fixed', especially if it is just the yard that is being remodelled. For those who are beginning from scratch and are happy to work with this 18in wide formula, however, the question remains as to what kind of background scenery might be squeezed into the remaining three inches or so beyond the loop line.

This immediately poses a more basic question of where the station is located within the imagined geography surrounding the layout. There are almost infinite possibilities and each modeller should have already made up their mind. For those still at the stage of planning and dreaming, here are a few suggestions that can be constructed quickly and easily. The rapidly expanding ranges of card kits and scratch-build aids will probably solve most problems.

NON-RURAL SETTINGS

Inner urban: This could be the backs of factories or warehouses, with small backyards between the low relief structures and the railway fence. Further along (looking left to right) these could give way to tenement backs or the rear of terraced cottages.

Inner suburban: Here one would expect a few trees and perhaps the back of a church or chapel, a cemetery or small park. Any house backs would belong to the larger Victorian/Edwardian properties and might even include the rear of a public house.

Outer suburban: Now the house types would be newer and probably include the more familiar semis of the 1920s and '30s. Some could be similarly styled bungalows with flower and/or vegetable gardens, even though there isn't much space to model them, and also more greenery.

On all the above it's a value judgement as to how much space is available for a low bank, cutting-side or level verge between the edge of the refuge loop and the boundary fence. If one wished to keep the whole exercise extremely simple, then just add a narrow verge beyond the fence and use the remainder as a road to the station, modelling it with street furniture, lights and appropriate period vehicles.

RURAL SETTINGS

Since our yard is relatively small but straggles a bit, a rural background may be more appropriate. Surprisingly there are many possible variations, especially for those who are more scenically inclined. Many wayside stations were a long way from the small towns and villages they served. It might be true to prototype to simply model the regionally appropriate farming activity beyond the fence, while taking the seasons into account.

It was not unusual for small communities to grow up around the station. While still modelling the backs of buildings beyond the fence, these could include a pub, the stationmaster's house, railway cottages and maybe a garage or scrapyard.

Terrain can be visually interesting in its own right. Cuttings can be used to good advantage, both for simplicity and for speed or cost. Grass banks should have a slope of roughly 45 degrees; in this period they would be largely free of vegetation apart from the odd gorse bush or small shrub. The slope will determine the maximum height to which one can work: three inches, or at the most four, will place the cutting top at the absolute rear of the layout. The sheer face of a chalk or limestone cutting, however, gives greater scope for height and leaves more space on top for scenic development.

Boundary fences would always be at the top of the cutting and may well have been in a particular house style: the Great Western, for example, favoured tall wooden posts with distinctively shaped tops and no fewer than eight unevenly spaced wire strands. Check available photos to see what is best for your needs. Every railway needs telegraph poles set along the tops of cuttings or on the slopes. Don't forget the wire stays, but think twice about putting on the cables themselves. Remember too that the insulators (or 'dolls') should always face towards London.

Many of the original companies were quite 'green' in their approach even a century or more ago. Certainly the GWR was renowned for planting pine-trees around and on the approaches to its rural stations. Initially these were intended to disguise this new scar on the landscape, but now they tower loftily above industrial estates and supermarket car parks, the original stations being but a distant memory. Some of these features can be seen on the completed project and on the photographs of my own layouts.

CONSTRUCTING A CUTTING

Construction of a cutting or a embankment relies almost entirely on 5mm foamboard formers with a thick paper or thin card lattice, covered with a mix of scenic mats, dried lint and paper towels coated with emulsion and ready-mixed filler. It is a very quick and relatively clean technique. Since it does not need to bear any weight it is also very light. You will, however, need to plan in advance where you intend to place any trees, telegraph or electric poles. Fence lines and poles can share the same route along the layout. This must always be formed by a vertical strip of foam-board so the 'legs' can be glued and pushed into place in the soft inner core. If the poles are to be sited on the slope of the cutting, they should be pushed into the vertical cross contours or into suitably fixed additional pieces of foamboard.

Trees can be treated more flexibly. The trunk must have a lengthy, securely fixed spigot protruding from the trunk. I normally use a length of 2mm diameter plastic rod or tube, often cut from cotton buds. At the site one needs to glue an upright tube with the same inside diameter. For a permanently sited tree the spigot is simply coated with plastic cement and pushed into the tube. If it is to be a portable layout where the trees need to travel separately, follow the above principle but add four or five 'roots' around the trunk from green-coated thin florist's wire. Plant the tree without gluing and bend the roots to unobtrusively follow the terrain surface. This may seem like overkill, but my trees, though lightweight, are often nearly a foot tall and can be equally broad at their bushiest. They do need that extra touch to ensure they remain upright and stable.

The scenic backdrop is simple to construct. The three subassemblies that make up the side of the cutting are shown in various stages of completion. At the front is the station-end portion with its latticework fully executed; the black play foam is in place and the tree sockets have also been fixed. Centre left and at the back are the next two portions with the recycled lint mostly fixed and the pastel shading in progress. The small recess on the right-hand section will accommodate the water crane for the refuge loop. There are two advantages from this approach: each section can be worked up away from the layout at the modelling bench and the combined weight of all three subassemblies is just 300g.

The trees for the project were made using the same method as that on my own two layouts and provided for a local club. They are simply the dried stems from sedum flowers, cut when they have gone to seed and then every tiny seed-head is snipped off. The stems are combined and bound together with fine florist's wire to best reproduce the chosen type and shape of the tree. The delicate twigs and branches can be brought into leaf using the appropriate foliage mats or teased out from carpet underfelt and various scatters. The trunks are coated with smears of plasticine subsequently painted with matt enamels, but do not use brown. A plastic or wood spigot is pushed into the base and securely glued. The completed trees, even when modelled to scale heights of more than 60ft (240mm), weigh only a few ounces and are easily 'planted' into their prepositioned tubes. If it is a solid baseboard you can use drilled holes instead.

THE BACKSCENE

In order to put the goods yard into a more realistic setting, I have modelled some landscaped background, constructed as three modules to sit at the back of each of the three track boards. If the yard were intended as part of a permanent home layout it would be much easier and far less complicated as there would be no need for separate sections. Each piece is built up on a simple base of mounting board, which would not be needed on a permanent layout. The contours and sub-frames are cut from 5mm foamboard and the lattice is scrap drawing paper. It can be assembled with any glue, but the quickest way is to use a hot-glue gun when all the components have been pre-cut.

The methods used are exactly as previously described. A single sheet of A2 drawing paper provided sufficient strips for the latticework. As it would not be required to bear any weight, there was no need for packing beneath the strips and the surface layer could go straight on. Rather than using torn strips of thin gauze or paper towels to form the terrain and then laboriously coating them with a mix of masonry paint and filler, I initially opted for my usual short cut of going straight to a grass-mat covering. On second thoughts, however, this seemed to offer too little that was new to the reader, so I went back to a technique used in the 1960s and '70s, when scenic textures were almost non-existent and modellers relied on dyed sawdust, cork granules or tea leaves. One method used then, though the results were unpredictable, was to glue lint 'fluffy-side' down on to a firm base, then rip off the backing to leave the fibres standing up. I always chose to glue the lint to my less than firm lattice right-side up, having pre-dyed it, and then use tweezers to tear up some of the fibres, before adding watercolour tones and pastel effects.

For the project, elderly fragments of lint from the scrap box were glued to the lattice with PVA, although any spray adhesive would do the job, and then brushed with green pastel dust in half-a-dozen different tones. The technique is quite similar to that needed when using a grass-mat in the same situation. It takes several dustings of different scenic dressings to bring a rather bland surface to life, but the results are good enough to exhibit.

My solution to the difficult problem of fencing is to find a simple piece of 1 x 2in strip wood about 30in long, drill holes along the top to give rows with different spacings to cope with the closer posts of the railway fence compared with the wider spaces used for the farm's barbed-wire fence. The holes should be large enough to accommodate fence posts from plastic kits, balsa or hardwood strip. For this project I have used household matches predrilled with five holes to accept nylon thread. The tops were cut at angles similar to the familiar GWR posts. They were modelled slightly taller than the correct scale-height to make the illustration more clear. This method is easy, versatile and cheap, but I would avoid using it for a GWR eight-strand wire fence.

Don't forget the stays on the telegraph poles. The thin thread is glued to a pin and simply pressed into the landscape to produce a taut appearance.

ABOVE: *You should now go over the whole layout with assorted scenic dressings and pastels. Remember to plant suitable weeds and undergrowth along the fence lines, around buffer stops, telegraph poles and lamp standards. Disguise any joins where buildings meet the ground.*

LEFT: *This is perhaps a glimpse into the future for this project as well as a test of its practicality. A slower goods working has been turned into the refuge loop to allow the more important Star-hauled train to overtake on the fast line. Meanwhile the yard is being shunted by the daily pick-up goods.*

CHAPTER FIVE

THE MARSHALLING YARD

THE MARSHALLING YARD IN THE STEAM ERA

In the previous section we looked in some detail at the nature, functions and operations of the goods yard. Before going into similar detail on the marshalling yard it is worth spending a few paragraphs on how they came about.

The growth of the railways and the expansion of towns and cities during the nineteenth century were not only simultaneous, they were completely intertwined and interdependent. The railways brought with them new opportunities for industry and commerce, generating yet more goods traffic and increasing passenger demand, which continued to feed off each other. By the 1890s both had become well established, creating the urban environments that are now so much a part of our economic and cultural heritage.

The smallish town once served by just a fairly simple goods yard had, in a few brief decades, become a sprawling city with a complex railway network with several passenger stations and an even larger number of goods yards and 'goods stations'. These handled all the local road/rail traffic for the city but, in addition, also served as interconnections between the various railways themselves. Part of the yard would be specifically dedicated to the loading and unloading of wagons for local customers, another area would include transfer sheds where loads were moved between vans for onward journeys, while the rest of the yard would see complete trains broken up and reassembled into new consists for other destinations.

These depots and yards, although originally constructed in relatively open country, were now completely surrounded by urban development. This obviously imposed severe limitations on any further expansion despite the ever increasing traffic demands. Something had to be done and it was obvious that the local and transfer facilities should remain where they were. But the reassembly of the complete trains, for which the depot was just a convenient location, could be done somewhere else and that became the role of the marshalling yard.

THE EVOLUTION OF THE YARDS

The extensive complexes required for marshalling yards could be quickly established outside the main urban area where land was still relatively cheap. They were large and sprawling affairs but, given a fairly flat piece of land, the loops and sidings could be laid cheaply, economically and without significantly affecting either traffic flows or the local populace. Once they were operational they would be able to receive, reassemble and dispatch complete trains often in just a few hours. They could work around the clock, if necessary, and required little in the way of facilities and apart from that needed for their own operations. At a stroke they would serve their own precise function while the vacated space on the inner-city yards would now permit their required expansion.

There were, albeit in somewhat simple terms, three types of yard. The most impressive were the huge hump yards, which were a comparatively new innovation and were almost fully automated, but their sheer size makes them impossible to model. Next in size were the large bi-directional yards, which could, as the name implies, receive and dispatch trains from both the up and down routes. These could make a modelling venture, but they would require a very large space to do them justice.

The most typical form covered those yards which dealt with traffic in only one direction. These

Many marshalling yards owe their origins to the Second World War. Some were constructed, or at least planned, in response to the increased political tension in the late 1930s. Others were still further expanded as part of the preparations for the launch of the Second Front. South Moreton Sidings (generally known as Moreton Yard) falls into both categories. It was completed in 1940/41 and expanded in 1943, due to its key location on the routes to the eventual D-Day embarkation ports. The photograph clearly shows its remote site and the scale of the earthworks involved even on relatively flat terrain. NATIONAL RAILWAY MUSEUM

can be modelled in a reasonably sized layout room, perhaps a garage, loft or large bedroom. They could be either up or down yards and many major stations would have one of each located at opposite ends of the town. Their role and operations were simple and involved nothing more complicated than receiving complete trains, breaking them up and reassembling the wagons into new trains to work forward to their eventual destinations or to another yard for further shuffling.

LOCATIONS AND LAYOUT

These yards could be very different in appearance. The earlier ones, although originally laid out in open country. Would by this time be surrounded by more recent urban expansion. Instead of green fields and hedgerows they would now be flanked by the backs of houses, industrial buildings, trading estates and power stations. The newer sites, many of which were built or substantially altered during the Second World War, would still have a rather raw look about

Moreton Yard was busy right up to the end of wagonload traffic in the late 1960s. This view is taken from the departure end where the long goods-loop joins the up-lines to Reading and beyond. Note how almost every siding is filled close to capacity. The low chalk cutting provided a backdrop to the whole site. NATIONAL RAILWAY MUSEUM

them, perhaps with exposed earthworks separating the sidings from arable land or maybe outlying sports fields. None of these should provide too much of a modelling challenge. The yard itself would be little more than a lot of track with a couple of very basic buildings, much like a real-world interpretation of the modeller's fiddle-yard.

The yard had no public access, which perhaps is one reason for the scarcity of photographs, and so needs no entrances or facilities beyond those absolutely necessary for its day-to-day operations. The only building of any significance would be a single-storey block containing accommodation for the enginemen, shunters and maybe the local gangers, with perhaps a small office for paperwork. There would need to be a water supply for the yard-pilots and visiting engines, and this in turn might require a water tank and maybe a small pumping station. Signalling within the yard, however, would be minimal. If it was sited alongside a busy four-track main line, perhaps with an additional goods line, then this might be a convenient

place to have a signal box and some main-line signals. Apart from that, the only other features are the staff access road, some car parking, a primitive cycle shed and maybe a small coal heap.

OPERATING A SMALL MARSHALLING YARD

The yard would normally be worked by one or perhaps two small tank engines, referred to as yard-pilots. These would be supplied by the local shed or motive power depot (MPD) and would arrive, fully coaled and watered, via the relief or the goods line. If there was any local traffic from the station yards, this would be brought down with them. They would then spend the entire shift shunting the yard with occasional visits to the staff block to refresh the enginemen and top up the tanks. These pilot-rosters were usually in the hands of veteran ex-main-line drivers, who were likely to bang the wagons around as quickly as possible to gain extra minutes in the crew-room. At the end of their shift they would await

No suitable images of Moreton at the time have been found. The photographs shown here were all taken in the early 1960s from a vantage point on the overbridge situated just west of the yard. Fortunately the camera angle provides tantalizing glimpses of the busy sidings. The passing express is from Paddington to Hereford and will take the avoiding line at Didcot heading north via Oxford. BEN BROOKSBANK; LICENSED FOR REUSE UNDER THIS CREATIVE COMMONS LICENCE

This time it's a through-goods that commanded the cameraman's attention, so there is some inspiration and information in the main subject as well as in the distant view of the yard. BEN BROOKSBANK; LICENSED FOR REUSE UNDER THIS CREATIVE COMMONS LICENCE

the arrival of their reliefs before returning to the shed and clocking off. If the shunters were on the same shifts and lived near the shed it is more than likely that they would hitch a lift on the footplate or with the guard if traffic was attached.

Incoming goods workings would arrive either off the relief line or from the goods line, if this could be accessed further back. They would be routed onto the reception loop and the locomotive detached. It might require a top-up, especially if working forward with a freshly made-up train; if not, it would return to the shed for servicing, running tender-first light engine, if necessary. If the yard or the main lines were busy, it might be held out of the way before coupled to other incoming engines to save on movements. Immediately the train engine was released one of the pilots would draw the wagons back up the head-shunt and then propel them onto one of the reception roads to begin their splitting up. This cleared the loop for the next arrival.

The yard would be laid out with a ladder of sidings progressively called from 'Number 1 Road', nearest the loops, out to the last one usually termed the 'back road' or 'cripple road'. The first one or two roads were always reception sidings, while the back road was used to park wagons that were either damaged or had hot-boxes and couldn't proceed. It was also used to park spare brake vans.

The main group of sidings were allocated to the various destinations further along the route; these might be specific stations if the traffic was justified, junctions and the stations they served or simply the next yard along. As each of these became vacant, the first shunt was for the pilot to retrieve a brake van and move it up to the stop-block. Meanwhile the shunters, who were always the men in charge, would be walking the newly arrived train and identifying where each wagon and van was to go. If their counterparts back up the line had done their jobs properly, the local men could then immediately uncouple the 'cuts' intended for each particular road. If the wagons were all mixed up, then their job became that much harder and the yard pilot became far busier.

The shunters would usually work in pairs led by a senior man; a busy yard would have several sets, each on specific roads. This may seem labour intensive, but

Another freight heads west and gives a further opportunity to study its consist as well as the traffic in the yard. BEN BROOKSBANK; LICENSED FOR REUSE UNDER THIS CREATIVE COMMONS LICENCE

yards were sprawling affairs and it was far more efficient to have the men working a few adjacent roads than trying to race from one end of the yard to the other. The footplate crew were little more than the tools with which the shunters did their job and it was down to them to get it right. Instructions were no more than a series of whistles and hand signals, or flickering oil lamps in the dark, and it was down to the driver and particularly his fireman to react quickly. The job was always pressured and frequently dangerous and it is not surprising that shunters were among the better-paid employees. Shunting was carried out at speeds all too rarely seen on model layouts and a real-life shunter needed to be fast on his feet and nimble of wrist to pin the brakes on a fast-rolling cut of wagons.

As soon as a road neared completion a fresh engine, if required, would come down from the shed ready to work it forward. If the relief was clear it could pull straight out and proceed on its way, but there was usually a lengthy stretch of loop line on which it could be held without obstructing the work in the yard.

Marshalling yards were simple in concept but complex in their operation. There is potential for a fascinating model. To illustrate this I have chosen to base a theoretic layout on the one known as South

Moreton Sidings or Moreton Yard. This is about a mile east of Didcot Junction on the Bristol–Paddington main line. The railway here has pairs of fast and relief lines together with a separate goods line between the station and the yard. It was considerably extended in 1943 to handle the extra military traffic associated with the Second Front and it remained busy until the decline of wagon-load operations in the post-Beeching 1960s. The choice was decided not just because I am a staunch 'Western' man and grew up just a few miles away, but it was also the only one I could find for which there was both reference material and photographs.

MODELLING THE MARSHALLING YARD

This will be a different sort of project as there is no actual building involved and no new techniques to be mastered. Instead it is an exercise in armchair modelling. The yard itself is little more than a large number of probably parallel tracks, all connected by an equal number of points. It makes for a project full of contradictions, providing the ultimate viewing platform for a lavish collection of goods stock and an equally broad range of freight and mixed-traffic locomotives. Another positive feature is that it offers the operator almost limitless potential for 'prototypical' shunting and freight movements. The obvious downside, that it needs a lot of space, is exactly the problem faced by the real railway. While the railways could exercise some flexibility in both the location and the attendant costs of construction, the modeller must live within his constraints. Nonetheless the prospect remains alluring, despite the obvious difficulties, so it is worth investigating what space is available and how we might plan a yard that appears realistic and workable.

RESEARCH

The starting point is, as always, research. In this case it is completely restricted to desk research as there are no yards remaining to enable any worthwhile fieldwork. Even this will not be easy as little material is readily available. Very few photographers

Looking the other way, west towards Didcot, shows an approaching freight on the separate goods line leading down from Didcot. This kept the main lines free of slow-moving goods trains and allowed them to have easy access to the yard. This is a feature that will be examined when we consider Moreton as a modelling opportunity.

bothered with these sites: they were not attractive locations and offered little in the way of dramatic photo opportunities. Some pictorial evidence, however, is to be found, even if it is only as background to a more interesting subject. The research can at least be given some useful parameters within which to concentrate one's efforts. The first thing is to establish a very loose outline of the back story, which need be little more than a rough idea of the geographic location and the company or region that operated there. If by some chance relevant information is available, copy everything that may be of use. If you can't find anything, here are a few suggestions on what to look for in a more general sweep, remembering to take good-sized copies of anything vaguely useful:

- The sizes of typical yards, their layout and the number and length of the sidings.
- The amount and type of stock in view.
- The typical traffic handled and its frequency.
- The loco types used as yard pilots.
- The loco types arriving or departing with trains.
- The facilities, including water cranes/tanks, offices, mess rooms, signal box/signals and coal heaps.
- The general background, such as industrial, trading estates, house backs, agricultural and earthworks.
- The nature of the adjacent lines: main, relief, goods loops and so on.

In addition to the many albums that may have provided some of the above information, autobiographies by footplate men and other railway servants can be a useful source. As well as being good reads in their own right, they can offer a vital sense of the real atmosphere of the working railway in the days of steam and may perhaps yield some extra photographs for your file.

The old-fashioned 2.5 inch to the mile Ordnance Survey maps, if you can locate them, show the various track layouts in astonishing detail. Even if you can't find the exact one you want, any examples showing a marshalling yard will be helpful. Lastly, a sweep of the internet could well throw up a relevant signal box diagram; although not to scale, these can at least show the basic layouts, together with the adjacent main lines.

PLANNING

The forms of research listed above will be of assistance in your planning as well as suggesting how the layout might operate once built. It is now time to start the all-important planning phase, following the same path as in the previous projects. Start by making preliminary pencil plans on a scrap pad and refining these to more scale drawings on graph paper. The optimum design is then transferred to a half-size plan on several sheets of A1 or A2 paper stuck together to accommodate the whole job. There are naturally some critical factors that must be taken into account at every stage:

Available space: This is obviously finite. No matter where the layout will be built – shed, garage, loft or spare room – there will be doors, windows,

obstructions, headroom and access to consider, in addition to the overall shape and dimensions. All of this must be plotted accurately and to scale if the outcome is to be successful.

Layout space: The amount of space for the actual baseboards will be governed at its outer limits by any of the features listed above. You should, however, also consider the inner limits, which must take account of operator space and access, ease of access to all parts of the layout, and the optimum sizes of the yard itself and the essential fiddle-yard/storage sidings. At the graph paper stage this can just be pencilled in and confirmed when more details become clear.

Train lengths and siding space: This is ultimately down to each modeller. Unless you are very fortunate and can afford a custom-built space, there is no point in even thinking about replicating the real thing. In-bound goods trains could well exceed eighty wagons with a large freight engine at the head; these

The version of a marshalling yard squeezed into the 'Wessex Lines' layout is far from a perfect solution, but it just about fits in a 6 x 2ft space and provides more than 20ft of sidings.

would need the reception-loop alone to be more than 30ft (9m) long with similar provision in the sidings and fiddle-yard. For the purposes of this exercise it is best to work to our previous maximums of around seventeen four-wheelers and a loco, which would require around 6ft (1.8m), plus an allowance for clearances.

Minimum radius: There are two aspects to be looked at: the visual appearance of the track, particularly on the main-line approaches; and the necessary evil of trying to pack as much as you can into the space available. Most currently available r-t-r goods engines are quite happy on 2ft-radius curves, which are just about acceptable visually for work on the main line. However, the actual space required for this and its associated point-work will be larger as the outer tracks will then be closer to 30in-radius. The yard itself is less of an issue as the small tank engines on pilot duties can cope with short-radius points.

PLANNING IN PRACTICE

The next stage is to put some of the theory discussed into practice. The following examples are either based on or inspired by the marshalling yard at South Moreton. This was not just a random choice, but it fulfilled most of the research criteria and had the additional advantage that I knew it from my days as a spotter in the early 1950s. To take the argument one step further, if I were ever in a position to build such a layout, then Moreton would be the certain choice. I believe that the following exercise is firmly rooted in a sort of reality.

The first step is to summarize the results of the research (see table below):

As you can see, the research covered all the necessary aspects and produced valuable additional details about the destinations for the onward traffic. Most had their own numbered sidings working out from the reception roads (1 and 2), including Hayes, Maidenhead/Slough, Basingstoke, Sonning Power

Location	GWR/BR (W), Berkshire, 1m E Didcot, up-yard, 4track main line, goods line
Size	10 later 16 sdgs, recept, loop(s), 60/90 wagons, head-shunts etc [built 1941 ext. 43]
Occupancy	mostly close to capacity
Traffic	mixed, ex S. Wales, Sdn./Chelt., Oxf., Midlands, N. West and trip-wkngs
Pilots	ex Did. Panniers and occ. 61xx
Visiting	28xx, 30xx, 49xx, 0-6-0s, Black 5, 8F 2-8-0s, H15, S15, Moguls, occ. BB/WC
Facilities	sig.box, PW hut, oil hut, coal, water crane(s) and WW2 acc. block
Background	o'bridge approach, cutting dept., low chalk cutting behind, arable farmland
Main lines	[outward] goods/up-rel./dn-rel./up-fast/dn-fast
Sources	GWJ 90, Didcot Engineman, Harold Gasson, GW Echo and personal visits

Station, Southern Railway via Reading, Tonbridge, Feltham, Redhill, Taplow and three different yards in Reading. The enormous modelling potential is apparent, even though it is impossible to cram it all in. A very reasonable compromise on a reduced scale can capture the essence of the yard and still produce more than enough activity to occupy the average operator.

CHECKING THE FIT

The next stage is to see how much might be accommodated in a decent-sized space. You may find, however, that it would still be too much for the smaller rooms of modern houses, though it might squeeze into the garage.

The initial sketches and squiggles are developed into two different interpretations during the graph paper stage. One represents the ultimate in ambition with the full four-track main line as an independent continuous run, which would satisfy my love of watching through workings on this principal route. The second is a simplified version reducing the main line to just two tracks, but still retaining its continuous run and independent operation, and it might prove possible to squeeze it into a smaller space. The aim on both schemes is to maximize the length of the sidings and their balancing lengths in the fiddle-yard loops, while also permitting realistic shunting moves and sensible rail access from the goods and relief lines. Where possible the point-work on the through lines is maintained as medium-radius, although in the yards it may need to be reduced to the short version. All the points are available in the usual Code 100 form and all three eventual layouts need to make use of the full range.

If it appears that these layouts are not fully defined, this is inevitable as they have not been subjected to the next phase: the half-size floor plan. Since we are only dealing with a theoretical project, rather than fully modelled goods shed and goods yard described in Chapters 3 and 4, there is little to be gained by going any further. For those who are sufficiently enthused to proceed to these next stages, I would suggest an interim plan redrawn to a more exact scale on the very largest sheet of 1mm grid graph paper that you can obtain. Unfortunately large sheets of this type are difficult to source even from the major office equipment suppliers. These planning stages, however, are the best time to discover and correct any poten-

There is some shunting in progress and two engines have arrived ready to take charge of the next out-bounds. They are being held on the up loop line and so remain clear of the running lines and the yard. Unfortunately there was insufficient room for a head-shunt beneath the overbridges and on the adjacent board. The shunting moves frequently intrude onto the up main line.

This is the view from the other end of the yard with an in-bound goods waiting in the up-loop. The loops are very short with a limit of about eight wagons. In some cases the train engine will draw them forward and set them back on to the long reception siding; on other occasions it will uncouple and return light-engine, tender-first to the shed using the down-main or down-loop. The four-arm shunting signal is, like all the others on 'Wessex Lines', made from Ratio kits but based on real examples. This one is from Abergavenny.

tial problems and, if you are able to work at a larger scale, it then becomes easier to spot the snags. If you are unsuccessful in finding any, draw a simplified but accurate grid on an A1 scrap pad or mounting board and work on that.

SOLO OR TEAM EFFORT?

The concept for both schemes is that they are intended for the solo modeller and permanent layouts at home. The ideas and most of the plans, however, could easily be adapted for exhibition use and for multi-operator presentation. The operating wells would certainly accommodate more bodies and the scenic area can be left as planned. However, for public viewing the existing back-scene would need to come off and a simplified and lower version installed on the inside. This would mean that the operators were in view but, given the immense variety of trains that could be run on the four through tracks and the constant movements in the yard, I think this would be a small price to pay. The number and variety of the services is only limited by the amount of stock available on the layout and that which could be substituted at short notice.

This would make it an ideal project for a small group of like-minded friends or for the exhibition team within a club. Since the actual real world location saw GWR/BR (Western) locomotives from all over the region together with LMS/BR (Midland) and SR/BR (Southern) examples, most tastes should be catered for. This mixture of companies and regions is not just confined to freight

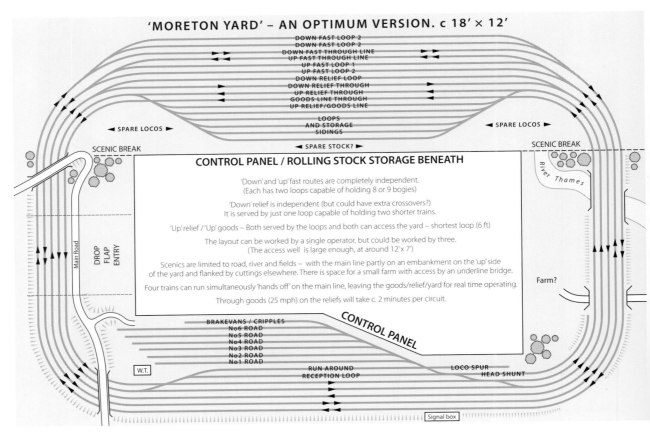

This is a possible track plan for Moreton. It would be ideal for a large bedroom, garage or custom-built shed. As a club layout it could also provide plenty of operating potential on club nights or on the exhibition circuit. All the key elements have been included, together with some suggested scenic features.

engines. There were numerous inter-regional passenger workings with reciprocal stock and many 'specials', including LNER/BR (Eastern) examples coming down from the north.

THE END-TO END MODEL

Having now firmly established Moreton's credentials as a basis for a continuous-run layout, it is worth examining if it could possibly translate into an end-to-end layout. I am well aware that many modellers don't have a large spare room or convenient empty garage, in which case the single-sided plan is the only option. Yet even this version will still take up quite a few square feet. The very minimum width must be at least 24in (30in would be preferable), but the real difficulty is the length. I found it almost impossible to achieve a workable scheme in less than 22ft (6.7m). This might be quite generous if the model were a terminus and only needed a fiddle-yard at one end, but a marshalling yard requires two: one for arrivals and the other to represent their onward destinations. That problem is made worse by the desire to operate reasonably long goods trains, even if they are shorter than the seventeen four-wheelers with which we have been working.

In the third diagram I have drawn an initial plan that could be built along the wall of a garage. It has a 10ft (3m) section to accommodate the yard, which I hesitate to term the 'scenic section', flanked by a pair of 6ft (1.8m) traversers or cassettes. Viewed from the back wall towards the operator, the track plan reads: goods/relief, reception loop/head-shunt, and six or seven sidings. The through roads, which would have been rather pointless in an end-to-end scheme, have had to go.

The emphasis is on the operation of the yard. Unfortunately there is no alternative other than to physically carry the goods stock from the full/destination-traverser or cassettes back to their starting point at the other end. However this is all 'one man's railway' and, as long as its inherent shortcomings are acceptable, it can make a workable layout. One idea to consider is that the height of the layout might influence the available width: if it could be constructed closer to eye level,

and thus clear the car roof and doors, it might be possible to gain a few extra inches. The actual dimensions of the garage, the car and the layout are completely inter-related. No doubt the keen modeller will know where their priorities lie and will utilise every spare inch. If, for example, there is some extra room at the back of the garage that might permit a curved approach and a larger scenic area, then that second option would be a definite improvement.

OPERATING A 'MORETON YARD'

It is now time to look more closely at how such a layout might be operated. We will stay with the Moreton story and with a solo modeller running a home layout. As a starting point we will take it that everything has been assembled in the right place after the previous operations. Provided there were no night shifts, here is the likely scene that might greet us at the commencement of the working day.

The staff – the Yard Master, two senior and four junior shunters, one of whom is designated as the 'train meeter' – clock on at 6.00 a.m. In addition there would be a couple of workers from the Carriage and Wagon Department and the resident Moreton gangers. In the yard itself one would expect to see the reception loop and siding empty of traffic; the remaining sidings would hold various partly made-up trains of mostly short-wheelbase four-wheel wagons and vans, with many of the opens running sheeted. These rakes must be sufficiently short to allow the incoming stock to be coupled-on. If there is an empty siding it is likely to be the one for Sonning Power Station's coal supply. The back or cripple road might hold a few damaged or cast-off wagons and some spare brake-vans from the previous day's workings.

Turning now to the fiddle-yard and storage loops, those for the independent 'fast' main lines can hold whatever through passenger or goods trains we want to run. These might well include the 'up' 'Red Dragon' from Carmarthen or the 'Bristolian', alongside the

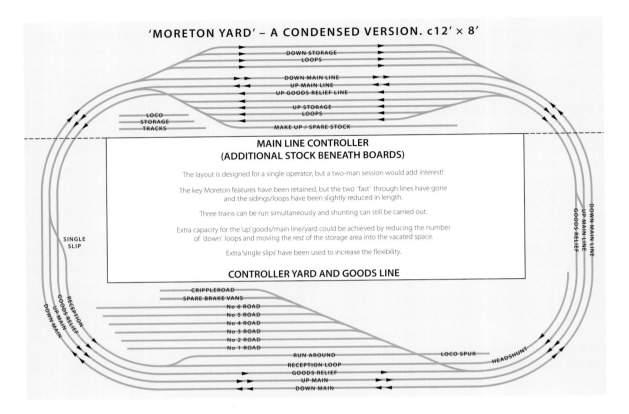

This simplified interpretation of Moreton could be accommodated in a smaller space. Some of the main-line atmosphere has had to be sacrificed but the operating potential remains intact.

'down' returning milk empties and a semi-fast for Oxford. More important are the goods loops, as these must hold the first of the morning's workings from the rest of the system.

The thing to remember is that these loops should at no time hold more stock than can be accepted at the yard and each road must be cleared to allow entry by the subsequent departure workings. It will no doubt take a bit of practice to judge this correctly or perhaps detailed workings on the scrap pad should provide an effective answer. When arranging these out-bounds, don't forget to allow for and include the appropriate train engines.

The records show that Moreton would usually receive up to twenty trains a day, although this varied, as did their length. The arrival times could also vary since most goods workings were of lesser importance and could be held to allow

passenger or more priority fast vacuum-fitted freights to overtake. The following lists of arrivals and departures are at best sequential and are neither timed nor even absolutely certain, but they are sufficient for our purposes (see table on the opposite page). Where possible notes on their consists have been added.

This pattern would continue for the rest of the day, but this is probably sufficient information given the length of the storage and yard loops and the time the operator would want to spend on a session. Not included are several of the resultant light-engine movements. These could be locos coming off trains from the west and north, which would return tender-first via Didcot shed. There would also be Southern locos returning home, also via the shed, after being turned and serviced. On the plan all these movements would use the goods line.

Typical Activity at Moreton Yard

Arr yard pilots — two panniers, ex Didcot shed (The modelled yard is considerably smaller and one engine would suffice – 57xx or 94xx)

Arr ex Oxford — mixed traffic – loco back light engine to Didcot

Arr ex Oxford — mixed traffic – drop off and pick up – loco to shunt then dep Reading

Arr ex Sonning — 61xx with spare SR brake vans – arrives via down relief and sets back – loco light engine to Didcot

Arr ex Bristol — 'The Cocoa' – vans from Frys drop off and pick up –loco to shunt then dep to Reading

Dep to Slough — mixed – 4 to Maidenhead, 12 to Taplow, to Slough

Dep to Taplow — mixed – traffic for High Wycombe branch

Arr ex Alexandra Dock — Welsh coal – (Sonning?) – drop off to Old Oak Common

Arr ex Severn Tunnel — mixed traffic from South Wales

Arr ex Bordesley Junction — mixed traffic

Arr ex Banbury — mixed traffic drop off and pick up for Basingstoke

Dep to Reading — 61xx with mixed for SR

Arr ex Didcot — 15xx War Department traffic from Ordnance Depot

Dep to Redhill — SR loco working back from Didcot

Arr ex Cardiff — mixed traffic

Arr ex Severn Tunnel — stops on loop to change crews only – dep to West Drayton

Dep to Basingstoke — mixed traffic

Dep to Basingstoke — mixed traffic ex Banbury

Dep to Didcot — 15xx return traffic for Ordnance Depot

THE CASSETTE SYSTEM

The cassette system permits the maximum number of sidings (10) and uses the reception/destination cassette as a head shunt.
With a single operator this is no problem as it is not needed until the re-formed departure.

With 'six foot' cassettes in use 16/17 4-wheel wagons can be run, but care must be taken when transferring them back to despatch.

THE TRAVERSER SYSTEM

The traverser system reduces the capacity. However, it is somewhat easiear and quicker to use. It should be possible
to combine a limited number of cassettes with the traverser. If so, this would assist in transporting the stock back from reception to despatch.

Extra sidings could be laid on the far side of the reception loop?

One reception road must be kept empty and aligned as a headshunt.

Note. More calculations will be necessary to determine the exact profile and number of tracks for the traversers.

A marshalling yard is not the ideal subject for an end-to-end layout. The actual yard is not the problem, but the inherent need to have extensive storage sidings at each end. The only answer that I could come up with, and which might fit along a garage wall, is to lose the main through lines and just keep the goods line. Even so the use of whole-train cassettes or lengthy traversers is essential.

STOCKING THE LAYOUT

It is necessary to calculate the amount of stock that could safely be accommodated for the average session. Excluding the four through lines, there are six sidings and six storage loops, which vary in length from 6ft and 7ft (1.8–2.13m). In order to have some room to manoeuvre, I would suggest that eighty or ninety four-wheelers are sufficient for the storage roads, while the yard should have not more than half that number. There is very little evidence of the exact ratios of the traffic handled at Moreton. The few photographs, however, underline the simple fact that open wagons vastly outnumbered all other types.

The overall stock lists suggest a ratio in the order of five to one, but this can be adjusted and still remain realistic while delivering the added advantage of greater visual appeal. For a start, at least a third of the opens should run sheeted, including both five-plank and seven-plank versions. A significant number can be dedicated to coal traffic conveyed in both steel and wood-bodied wagons. Further vans can be added to the stock list and these might be seen on the through services stopping to pick up and drop off or simply stopping to change crews. Van traffic would certainly represent much of the total consist coming in from Didcot Ordnance Depot and could well be seen in larger numbers on trains from Bristol. Perhaps a more appropriate ratio might be four-to-one or seven-to-three; to these key figures can be added a few specialist types such as cattle, lowmacs/bolsters, oil tanks and flats with containers or other loads.

MOTIVE POWER

The locomotive allocation, again excluding the through lines, can be as generous as you like and there is provision to park spare engines beside the loops. The incoming trains from the Western should definitely include 28xx, 30xx, Moguls, Halls, Granges and possibly WDs or Aberdares These could also provide the power for some of the departures. The pilots and trip-freights will be Panniers or Dean/Collett 0-6-0s. The through services can have any of these, plus of course the Castles and occasional Britannia or King. Arrivals from the north can also be headed by Western engines, but the ubiquitous Black 5s and 8Fs would also appear; these might sometimes also be glimpsed on the main lines. The options for Southern power are again wide open, but I would suggest that Moguls, Arthurs and Light Pacifics would be the most common. If you can track down a kit for the Western Aberdare and 15xx Pannier, you could then add interest to the Southern choices by looking for an N15x 'Remembrance' or an S15 (a Hornby r-t-r version is announced for 2016). The through lines would certainly see Light Pacifics, Lord Nelsons and maybe even a Merchant Navy on returning sets of both Western and Southern coaches. If a representative of the LNER is wanted, then an 'excursion' of Gresley or Thompson stock with a B1 or B17 at the head should fit the bill.

Modellers who might wish to create a setting more typical of the later years of the chosen period will still find plenty of r-t-r locomotives to replace the earlier versions. The shed pilots would be unlikely to change, but the trip-freights could be handled by Standard 2MT 2-6-2 tanks or the attractive little 78xxx class 2-6-0s. The arrivals would be headed by the Standard 4MTs or 5MTs, with perhaps one of the big 2-6-4 Standard tanks on services from Oxford or any out-bounds to Reading. The heavier coal workings from Wales or the north would see the ROD 30xx and WDs replaced by the outstanding BR 9Fs.

CONTROL AND CONCLUSIONS

If the layout is on analogue DC control then it will be best served by several units. The plan is designed to allow up to five workings simultaneously: 'up' fast and relief, 'down' fast and relief, plus the goods line and yard. Any operator, no matter how competent, can only 'drive' one train at a time, hence the need for separate controllers for each of the four continuous through lines. The trains on these are simply set in motion at their appropriate speeds and left to trundle around until replaced by a subsequent service. This allows them to make the constantly changing spectacle that is typical of a major main line. While all this is happening the operator is then free to use the principal controller to work the goods line and the yard. Obviously the various arrivals, departures and shunting movements are sequential, not simultaneous. If the layout has state-of-the-art DCC, these restrictions do not apply.

This has been a project unlike the others described in the book: there is nothing to be built and no new skills to be learned. The marshalling yards were a vital part of steam-era goods operations and it is a subject that couldn't be overlooked. I also think it has the potential to make a fascinating model, both to plan and to operate, and hope it may have proved sufficiently interesting to inspire some modellers to try their hand. If it seems too daunting for a home layout, why not get a team together to create a show-stopping joint venture for the exhibition circuit?

CHAPTER SIX

AN INTRODUCTION TO SCRATCH BUILDING

I cannot recall when the term 'scratch-building' entered the vocabulary of model making, although it was probably in the mid-1960s or the early 1970s, alongside that other catch-all expression 'kit bashing'. Somewhere along the line it has become more than just a definition of an activity; instead it has become hyped into a sort of status symbol. In today's jargon, to describe something as 'scratch-built' is to ascribe to it an accolade of excellence – all too rarely deserved.

From the beginning I want to try to dispel any ideas about it being the 'zenith of modelling' and remove some of the mystique that surrounds it. In doing so, I must give due praise and credit to those modellers at the very top of our hobby whose loco-motives, rolling stock, buildings and scenery are truly out of this world. Spend a couple of hours at Pendon

or browse the pages of Model Railway Journal and you will soon see what I mean. It is the difference between the Premier League and those of us in the amateur levels of the game, still playing for fun while learning new skills.

Why do we bother to scratch build stations, sheds, cottages, farms or factories in the first place? We have already discovered that there are shelves full of kits or ready-to-plant structures out there that should more than cover all our requirements. Most of them can also be easily enhanced, converted or combined to better meet even the more specific locations. There are two simple reasons behind our decision. First, we can model a building that will fit our layout by size and style, rather than force the layout itself to fit some predetermined footprint and still have to work on the structure to customize it

Pendon is a gateway to a bygone world. Buildings that have been much altered or even demolished are recreated in exquisite detail with accuracy down to the last brick.

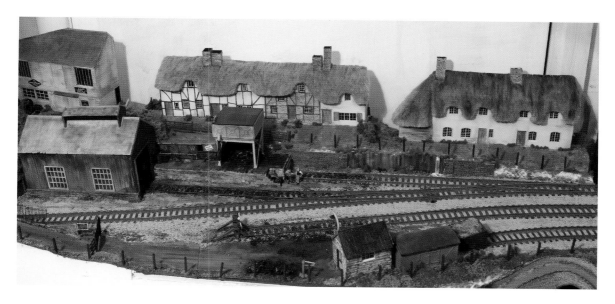

This small competition module had to be designed and built to fit within a precise area. All the buildings and structures, however, are built to scale from photographs of the originals.

to our desired style. The second is surely that same motivation that lies behind all good modelling, the urge to create something original for ourselves.

Benefits and Advantages

The advantages of scratch building are many and varied, as they allow us to:

- model something to exactly meet our space requirements.
- choose a building that appeals to us visually.
- respond to the urge to create something that has inspired us.
- set our own parameters for the finish and detailing.
- make best use of the available materials and accessories.
- tweak the structure to ensure optimum fit.
- develop new skills and improve our techniques.
- derive maximum satisfaction having done it all ourselves.

Even that list is not exhaustive. Above all, the overriding benefit is that we have total control of the project from start to finish.

THE SEARCH FOR ACCURACY

Another of the major myths surrounding scratch building is the vexed question of 'accuracy'. I fully accept that this is certainly an issue when applied to locomotives and rolling stock, which must be dimensionally correct and feature as much accurate detail as the modeller can achieve. Their starting points are works drawings , sheet metals, a well-equipped engineering workbench and considerable skill. That is truly scratch building, yet there are still many critical armchair modellers who will howl down a seemingly perfect model over a missing rivet on the buffer beam.

Buildings, though, are rarely subject to such criticism since the prototype information is invariably somewhat scarce. In our field dimensional errors, even of several millimetres, are almost unnoticeable. What is important is that the structure is properly square, verticals are vertical and the finished building looks right in its setting.

Before we get too involved in a small trial project, it is instructive to step back and look briefly at the levels of options that are open to the would-be scratch builder. It is probably easiest to start with the perfectionists. In relation to our theme of card con-

Scratch building enables the modeller to tweak the dimensions of a chosen prototype to fit the often smaller space available. Dainton Box on the author's 'Wessex Lines' has been reduced by a few millimetres to provide an appropriate subject for a very cramped and awkward site.

struction that, of course, means Roye England and his successors at Pendon Museum in Oxfordshire.

PENDON

Every model on the displays at Pendon is, as near as humanly possible, an exact reproduction of a real building. Field and archive research are used to produce all the required data, from the precise dimensions to the subtle changes of colour tones due to age and weathering. Each set of blueprints contains photographs, sketches, measurements, copious handwritten notes and even transcripts of interviews. The basic materials are high-quality card, watercolour paints, pastels and simple tools. Thatch is usually plumber's hemp, and other materials include various grades of paper and suitable glazing. They go so far as to scribe every individual brick or stone, even the broken ones, and each may receive at least half-a-dozen brushstrokes before it's finished. Many of the cottages include fully detailed interiors, right down to the correct paintings on the wall.

'PENDONESQUE'

This is my description of those who follow Pendon's example and methods to varying degrees of detail. They still aim for the best quality of construction and finish that they can achieve, ideally without recourse to any commercial components and accessories. Their materials and toolkits are largely similar but they are less likely to 'model to the half inch' and to scribe and paint each brick in the Pendon way. They may well have all the necessary skills and patience to join the museum, but the demands of their own layouts and projects impose constraints on their available time and space. They do not confine their modelling to exact prototypes but venture into 'typical' buildings to fit their layout's concept.

SCRATCH BUILDING USING COMMERCIAL AIDS

This is probably the largest group of all. Their modelling can include exact prototypes, modified prototypes, hypothetical or typical structures – in fact any subject that meets the requirements of their layout and for which at least some of the commercial aids are suitable. Their starting point remains the same: the design, drawing and preparation of the basic kit of parts. Their reference material may well come from personal field visits, photos and measurements, or from nothing more sophisticated than an illustration in a book or magazine. The finish on their models may be plain or textured brick papers,

This beautiful model of Packer's Smithy, King Charles Cottage and Ivy Cottage was lovingly crafted by Roye England as part of Pendon's 'Vale Scene'.

The author was born and grew up in Ivy Cottage, so it was perhaps inevitable that a scratch-built version would find a place on his 'East Ilsley' exhibition layout. The thatch is plumber's hemp and every tile is individually cut and laid. It is seen here on display at the museum as part of Pendon's fiftieth anniversary.

Tunnel Farm on 'Wessex Lines' is largely an invention, although inspired by Pond Farm in the builder's home village. It was built more than twenty years ago and was only made possible by relying on accessory pack windows, doors, gutters and drainpipes.

moulded plastic sheets, scribed filler or card treated with watercolour or acrylics. Use will be made of commercial glazing, etches, laser-cut frets, white-metal chimneys – indeed they will try anything that will save time and enhance the model to a greater degree than their efforts can achieve on their own. The increasing spread of computer-aided technologies, from complete 3D structures to simple downloaded prints, is already making an impact.

If we need a broad-brush definition to any and all of these activities, it amounts to this:'scratch building need be no more than creating your own basic kit, completing it in the method/materials of your choice, rather than buying a kit from a commercial source'.

SCRATCH BUILDING THE SMALL GOODS SHED

The very term 'scratch building' can be off-putting to those new to the hobby. The problem is that so many examples shown in magazines and at exhibitions come from the top end of the modelling tree. When encountering the outstanding contributions by the Pendon Museum team or such skilful individuals as Gordon Gravett or Dave Rowe, it is all too easy to say 'I could never do that!' Yet every scratch builder must start somewhere. The tools and techniques are no more difficult or complicated than those we have already explored when custom-

The very prominent mill complex on the 'East Ilsley' layout is based on a mix of actual and invented buildings. The mill itself still stands in Bridport and the small outbuildings come from Lyme Regis. Extensive use is made of Howard Scenics brick paper; the ventilators and sluice-gate gears are model-boat parts.

izing off-the-shelf kits. For those who choose card, or similar, as their medium, the assembly process is extremely simple and little different from that already encountered with the card-kits. Those modellers who elect to go down the 'plastic path' will face challenges that are rather more difficult and I can do no better than recommend anything written by Iain Rice or Dave Rowe. Above all, there is the huge benefit for the new modeller that it is modelling almost without rules and constraints. While you will be totally responsible for design and basic construction, there is a whole army of suppliers out there offering a wealth of components specifically as 'aids to the scratch builder'. It is up to each individual to decide how far they take the finishing of the model. My own efforts in this field reflect this. If I am building a rural cottage or a farmyard, I will tackle everything with the watercolours, except for the chimneys, gutters and drainpipes. If, however, the building is a railway structure, a piece of individual architecture or even a modern semi, then I will happily make use of the most suitable pre-printed brick, slate or whatever.

If the construction techniques are no more complicated than the average kit and all the finishes and accessories can easily be found, what makes scratch building so popular? It all lies in the initial creative phase from selecting the prototype, through planning out the kit and ultimately building that basic shell.

PREPARATIONS

The example chosen as an initial project will enable the modeller to test all of these aspects up to the completely self-finished model, with consideration of some alternative finishes via the trade. The building itself still exists and its exterior remains largely unchanged, although the inside has been extensively altered to serve a new purpose. Corfe Castle goods shed is on the very popular and ever developing Swanage Railway in Dorset. It is an ideal first time project as it is small, full of character and should fit on even the smallest layout. It has no 'through road' but simply the large doors to trackside and the loading bay opposite. This has the further advantage that it will give our kit greater structural reliability without the risk of a 'floppy' outer wall.

It was also an ideal subject for me since it is barely a half-hour's drive from home and a field visit was an easy option. a s a regular patron, 'all areas' access was quickly agreed. The visit followed the prescribed methods for obtaining the key information on dimensions, using both a measuring stick and a steel tape measure. The figures recorded were then supported by as many photographs as I considered necessary and further backed up by sketches and scribbled notes. I also checked whether any additional information could be found in my library, although on this occasion I was unsuccessful. The accompanying images from the excursion should help to give a good impression of the shed's structure, character and general appearance. If you intend to have a go at the project, I would recommend scanning these, together with any other useful ones in the instructions, and blowing them up to a 4 size. This will make them easier to manage as references while you progress through the various stages, as you will notice from my own use of this technique in this project.

This selection of elevations of Corfe Castle goods shed should help to provide the modeller with a clear impression of how the finished project should appear. As modelling aids they are best copied to A4 size for easier reference.

The results of the field research trip to Corfe provide the key components for this exercise in scratch building.

Start by assembling your visual aids, references and any measured or calculated dimensions. At this point I always find it worthwhile to make some preliminary working drawings. These help to give a better understanding of the building as a whole, how it might best be drawn in kit form and what snags may be encountered in the eventual process of cut and construct.

Select your A1 mounting board and cut off a suitably manageable section with scissors. The requirement is to be able to produce all the walls initially as a continuous piece of artwork. The approximate dimensions of the original are length 43ft, width 20ft and height 24ft, so the two sides and ends demand a total sheet size in our scale of not less than 600 x 100mm. The two half roofs also need to be considered. On some buildings one might possibly wish to include relief items like plinths or buttresses from the same piece of card. Taking these together, a segment or workpiece about 24 x 12in (600 x 300mm) should suffice in most instances.

SCALE DRAWINGS

It is now time to start on the scale drawing. Always work from the machine-cut edge upwards to ensure you maintain the essential horizontal. One should always aim to be able to bury the foundations of the building into the landscape. If the model is likely to be sited on a tabletop baseboard, however, as is probably the case here, then the deepest those foundations can be is to the tops of the sleepers, making a maximum of the underlay plus the sleeper depth of around 4mm. Using dividers set to 4mm, pin-prick the card and rule your building base line that distance in from the bottom of the card: that will be ground level.

I like to take full advantage of the machine cuts. Working from left to right, make the left-hand side the upright wall of the left-hand gable end as it will be when eventually viewed from the road side. Reset your dividers to the end wall width (78mm) and, using the data, pin-prick the card to produce the next corner and, checking with your set square, draw in the upright. Reset the dividers to the building length (172 mm) and pin-prick out from the datum line to produce the next corner. Draw in the upright, checking as you go, and then repeat the processes to draw the second gable and second side.

The next step is to draw the heights: along the eaves of the long sides and the ridge-point at the tops of the gables. My preferred method is to use the height of the eaves as another horizontal along the whole drawing. This is safer and ensures greater

The research results are translated into the artwork for the goods shed 'kit'. Some draft drawings may help you get in a bit of practice. Using the scrap areas for scribbled notes or measurements is also a useful technique.

accuracy than plotting the eaves individually. This is another exercise using dividers, this time set at 66mm from the ground-level baseline, Rule and draw it in faintly across the gables.

Turning our attention to the gable height (96mm), the first step, with the dividers again, is to draw an exact horizontal more or less centrally above each end wall. The centre is half the width of the wall and is thus 39mm in from the front corners. Set the dividers again and, measuring in from the corners, pin-prick the base line, the eaves line and the new top line. Connect them up with the set square; these should be exact perpendiculars.

The point where they cross the top line is now accurately placed as the ridge-point of the gable end. Once you are happy that all is well, connect these two points to their respective corners on the side walls. These lines, together with the line of the eaves and the final corner, can now be drawn in more firmly as they will become our eventual cutting lines

CREATING THE CORNERS

At this juncture you need to make an irrevocable decision. Your aim is to assemble a square box on which you can fix the two roof templates. You have

a choice here. The most accurate and most favoured method is to score and bend the four corners. This must be done on the reverse of the card and absolute accuracy is essential. The alternative is to prepare to cut the four sides into individual sections and then either mitre-join or butt-join them. Mitre-join is similar to the scoring process, but involves making two 45-degree cuts down to the exact fold points on the corners prior to bending. The mitre cut does exactly the same but on the two separated items. Both need practice: if it's your first time, carry out sufficient test cuts on spare card until you are confident enough to do it on the artwork. Butt-joins are no more than simple cuts made down the corner lines. You should be aware, though, that if you leave it at that your box will be either too wide, if you place the gable walls inside the long walls, or too long if the gables are to go on the outside.

Deciding which option you take is critical since the exact measurements of your roof template will depend on it. This raises the further choice of whether the two half roofs sit on top of the walls or inside them. The easy option, which also caters for a margin of error, is to let the roof sit on the walls.

If we choose score and fold or mitre-join then the measurements for each roof half can be taken from the eaves length and gable pitch length straight off the drawing. Where they will rest on the walls you can allow yourself a slight margin and cut to 1mm extra. You may also want to allow extra at the actual ridge of the roof on one half only, to allow the other to be a snug fit beneath it.

To return to the butt-join version, one option is to fit the side (long) walls inside the gable ends. This ensures that the roof must now follow the exact pitch you marked out. To maintain the correct overall dimensions you will need to cut the width of the card gable ends from each end of the long walls. Your roof measurements can be calculated exactly as above. At this point it is also worth re-marking the revised long wall vertical cuts, but don't cut anything yet.

COMPLETING THE DRAWING

There should be sufficient space on the piece of card for you to mark out accurately the two roof halves from the spare area above the eaves and between the gables, but double-check that is correct. Establish a new horizontal and measure out the dimensions, 178mm long and 48mm deep, with the set square and dividers. Absolute right angles are essential.

You now have all the key components of the basic kit. The two canopies were added later by the builders and it is best if you follow their example.

We can now turn our attention to drawing the doors and windows onto the artwork. The doors are identical in size and relative positioning. Their centres are exactly on the centrelines of the two long sides, so plot those centrelines first. The doorways themselves are slightly smaller and actually measure 10ft

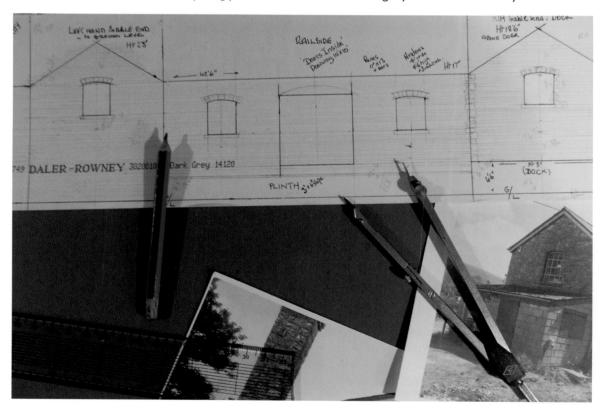

These are the very basic tools for drawing and measurement. I have found that a vernier scale, which can be calibrated down to hundredths of a millimetre, is far more accurate than dividers. It can be locked into position and the pointed jaws are sharp enough to mark card or plastic surfaces. Vernier scales are not necessarily expensive; this example cost just £7.

The artwork is now almost ready for cutting out. The horizontal rulings for the stone courses have been extended across all four walls, which would be the procedure if the whole building was going to be finished with painted stonework. They will be ignored for the project except on the south gable end.

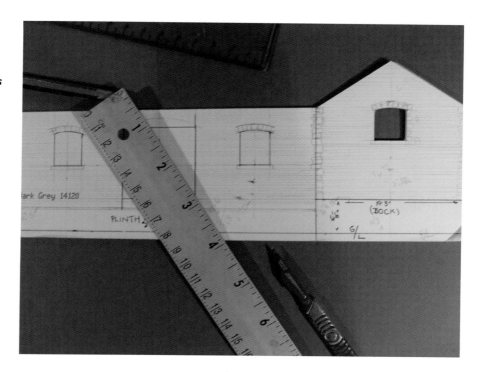

(40mm to scale) wide, 11ft 6in (46mm) high on the rail side and 15ft (60mm) to the top of the arch on the road side. Each side of the doors should therefore be 20mm from the centreline. The bottom of the doors is wagon-bed height on the trackside (this will ultimately be the floor height for the interior). Out on the vehicle dock side the bottom of the doors is at road level. Just to complicate matters, though, the lintels on both sides are at the same level. The aperture on the road side should therefore be 60mm from the base line and on the rail side it should start from 18mm up. I would suggest that you double-check this measurement against the actual levels of your wagon beds. Wheel sizes, track types and underlays will all have a bearing on the outcome. Draw these on the artwork clearly enough to make the cut lines obvious.

All the windows are the same size and are also symmetrical in their relative positions on the gable ends and rail side walls. Each one has an aperture of 16 x 16mm. On the rail side the centreline of each one is equidistant between the corners and the doorways. Draw these in, then divide the window widths by two and draw in those verticals exactly as

was done for the doors. They are the same height, 9ft 6in (38mm to scale) above the base line 9'6" (38mm). The horizontals for the sills can now be plotted. From these measure up the window height of 16mm, plus a couple of millimetres for the arch, and rule these as well.

The final two windows in the gable ends are tricky since they are identically positioned in relation to the pitch, but are at different heights from the surface. They thus require additional care. They are obviously on the centreline of the gable ends and these have already been drawn. We can therefore plot their widths at 8mm either side of that centreline. The height to the sills is the same at both ends, so we can use the obtained measurement from the south gable to fix this: it is actually 8ft (32mm) above the dock, which places the north gable sill at 50mm up from the base line. The two windows can now be completed in the same way as those on the rail side.

SCORING AND CUTTING.

The stage has now been reached when we could begin the cutting process. You can either choose to leave the largish piece of artwork as it is and begin to

When marking the initial score lines it is imperative to keep them exactly vertical and accurately placed. Errors at this stage will lead to problem corners when it comes to final assembly.

Cutting out the shallow 'V' groove for the 'score and bend' approach takes time, patience and considerable care. Any mistakes will lead to damaged artwork or fingers. Scalpels are sharp, so cut little but often and frequently test-fold the piece to ensure your groove is sufficiently deep but not too deep.

work up the eventual finish, or you start cutting out the structure and removing the door and window apertures. The first option retains the overall strength of the artwork's card, but at the expense of it still being fairly unwieldy and carrying bits that we do not yet need, notably the roof and all that surplus material. Cutting it all out to create the basic kit form, however, especially with those large doors and windows, will make it more vulnerable. Your earlier choice of whether to use score and fold, mitre joins or butt joins should also be borne in mind.

In this example I have settled on score and fold and cutting it out in full. I would, however, advise the modeller to avoid making the 'V' cuts too deep: as I have found to my cost, this renders the corners all too liable to breaking and tearing. With the work still intact, force a needle-point hole right through the card at the top and bottom of each of the corner lines. Turn the card over and join the needle holes to transfer that fold line. Using a metal ruler and a sharp new scalpel blade, make a series of diagonal cuts into the card with a ruler about 2mm out on either side of the fold line. You will discover, if you haven't already, that your mounting board is not solid but is in fact a series of laminates. Remove enough to give you more than a head start, but not so much as to make the structure start to bend and flex. Practising on a piece of scrap will show how far you should go.

Once you have treated all four corners, turn the card face up once again and, following the line with a steel rule, carefully cut right through all four sides of each large window and the two doors. If you can achieve a full cut through in a single pressured stroke, so much the better. One tip is to avoid cutting with just the scalpel point, but instead hold the instrument more 'flat' to make maximum use of the full blade. Invariably the corners of the apertures will remain uncut or only partially cut. Carefully lift the card and ease the blade right through to sever the remaining card until the centre drops out.

For the window arches it is just a question of patience. You can help by making a series of needle pricks almost through the card all around the curve, or simply go straight in with the scalpel point and

When performing the various cutting and scribing tasks, it's a good idea to keep your original images close by. Even the steadiest hand and sharpest scalpel are not error-proof. Arched windows and doorways are always high-risk areas and these constant reminders help to keep us out of trouble.

carefully carve the required shape. The arches are quite shallow, so the task is not too difficult.

The task of cutting out the finished artwork is straightforward: use the steel rule and 'flat' blade technique, and keep the cuts square. You can also cut out the two half roof templates and put them to one side.

DETERMINING THE FINISH

We have at last reached the point when the plain piece of cut-out card is transformed into a recognizable reproduction of the prototype. The decision has to be made how to finish the walls to best replicate what has been captured on our photo references. You must now choose whether to take up some of the trade offerings or continue down the DIY path. If there is a suitable pre-printed sheet available that would be the obvious choice. I would normally discount the inclusion of plastic sheets in either moulded or vacuum-formed versions. They are unlikely to exist in the Corfe style and are not the easiest of materials for a beginner to use, but I have finished one wall in plastic so you can judge for yourself.

There are several different approaches to the totally DIY finish. The easiest of these uses pencil and watercolours and it is worth looking at this in some detail. Using a ruler and squares and a soft sharp

pencil (B or cheap HB) draw on each stone course and each stone. If this building will rarely be viewed too closely, however, you need not get too bogged down with detail. Once done, use your palette to obtain variable mixes of mostly white but discreetly toned down with a touch of grey. Use a piece of scrap to test until you get what you want. The aim is always uniformity, but no two stones exactly the same. If you think from your test samples that the colour is right but the texture, or lack of it, is missing, try using a base coat of matt white emulsion brushed all over the walls. Better still, if you have any, use a coat of textured masonry paint or even plain masonry paint. A little additional surface interest can be had from a dusting of talcum powder while the paint is still wet. Once done, continue with the pencil and watercolours as above.

Rather than drawing pencil lines, you may wish to mark out the courses and stones with a sharp scribe, but avoid making this too deep or too wide: as you can see from photographs, at most distances any mortar courses are almost invisible.

For still greater definition you can try a fully coated surface. The simplest of these is to make up a kind of slurry using ready-mixed lightweight filler, PVA adhesive, a few drops of suitable emulsion paint and a measure of water. This should be just a fraction

This is the picnic-plate polystyrene finish, having been cut out and fixed to the north gable end (left hand) with normal PVA adhesive.

The basic one-piece kit comprising all the four walls that will fold together to make the simple box that is the shed. Whatever structure you are modelling, you will inevitably arrive at this stage. All the walls have had their respective finishes applied.

The polystyrene picnic-plate applied to the north gable end is very easy to work. All it takes is some light horizontal course-lines and careful drawing of the individual stones. Keep your visual references close to hand, but there is no need to slavishly attempt an exact copy. A 5H pencil is the only tool required and it must be sharp. Very little pressure will still give an excellent relief effect.

The embossed stone sheet used on the roadside wall was printed in distinctly North Country shades. It was given a couple of coats of white match-pot emulsion, but not so much as to obscure the relief detail.

too thick to apply with a soft brush, but it should still cover easily and quickly with a palette knife. A stiffer bristled brush would also do the job, but you run the risk of the brushstroke marks appearing too pronounced. A touch of grey watercolour will help tone down the whiteness of the mix. Then scribe or draw and paint as above.

The final choice is to use one of the air-dry clays available from most crafts shops. If possible, try to find the white version, which may be harder to track down than the more familiar terracotta colour. Apply it thinly and pre-brush the card with suitably liquid PVA to help adhesion. Sand down, if necessary, and complete using the scribing, drawing and watercolours as above.

The demonstration model has had each of its four walls treated in a different finish: simple draw and paint, the nearest embossed pre-printed card, a very approximate plastic sheet and, finally, a picnic-plate with drawn stones. The photographs are all in extreme close-up to enable readers to judge the method and results they most favour.

ABOVE AND BELOW: *The south gable end and the chimney were also marked out with the 5H pencil. This time it was worked in my usual method of drawing on top of an emulsion-painted surface. A degree of relief detail can be obtained this way, enhanced by further shading and highlighting with watercolours.*

The plastic-sheet version compares unfavourably with the poly-plate finish on the adjacent wall.
Even though this is one of the most widely used methods and can deliver outstanding results, I have
always found it laborious and no improvement on my usual techniques.

One important aspect of any building is the treatment of corners and window and door surrounds. This holds particularly true in the case of a relatively simple structure like Corfe goods shed. Attention to detail is all important and, since there is very little in the way of relief involved, this is best tackled as part of the overall surface finish.

WINDOWS

One skill worth learning is being able to recognize when you have reached a result that looks right. Invariably you will find that less is more and that overdetailing can just look silly. Bear this in mind when deciding whether the walls have been finished to your satisfaction, at which point it is time to look at the four windows. Once again it's worth seeing if there is a printed acetate with the correct dimensions or there might be a suitable etched brass sample, although this would need a white spray primer before glazing and installing. If not, you will need to resort to DIY again. My method here, aiming at simplicity

as always, is to transfer the window outline onto a piece of card and then carefully and accurately draw in the glazing bars.

Select your acetate or clear sheet and cut four pieces slightly over-size; an extra 5mm all around should be enough. Stick the pieces down on your drawing using masking tape to keep it firmly in place. Next, as a guide for the subsequent steps, very lightly scribe the outlines or glazing bars with a needle. Always use a steel rule and a steady hand. Do not score too deeply and avoid scratching the surface.

Depending upon what is to hand I use two different mediums. I prefer to use a mapping pen and drawing ink for the glazing bars and a thicker coat applied with a small brush for the wooden frames. I have also used 2mm strips cut from self-adhesive labels for the frames, sometimes carefully overlaying them to provide depth and contrast.

The other method is to replace the mapping pen and drawing ink with one of the readily available gel pens. These ballpoint types can be used with a ruler,

A vernier scale is the perfect tool for delivering the accuracy and precision needed when producing window artwork.

Keep the artwork securely taped down, as the slightest movement will destroy the verticals or the spacing of the glazing-bars.

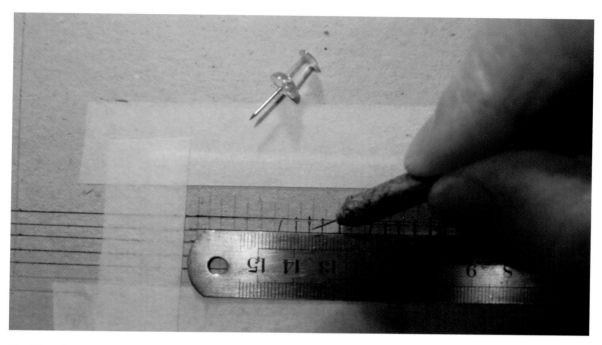

Scribing demands close coordination between hand and eye. I am using a needle-tool, but a map-pin or similar will also do the job. Keep the scribe tight to the ruler throughout.

The most difficult aspect of inking-in the scribed lines is the ink itself. The consistency must be absolutely right for a task for which it was not designed: too thick and it won't flow from the pen, too weak it won't produce the crisp white that is needed. Have suitable piece of scrap black card to hand, such as the reverse of your mounting board, and test before each application.

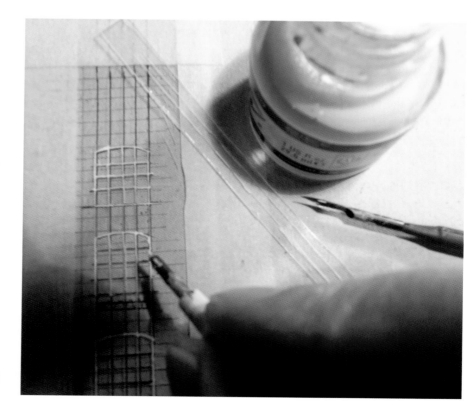

Ink on shiny plastic is easily removed and errors are therefore easy to correct. Something like a cocktail stick can be used to lightly scrape away any excess or blobs. Any omissions or poorly defined bars can be re-inked at the same time.

but they tend either not to flow at all or, worse, make blobs. Providing you can use a bit of scrap black card and a tissue you can keep the ink gel flowing and wipe away the blobs. If you make an error on one of the windows, make sure they are completely dry and then pick off the error with a sharpened cocktail stick, before re-inking the offending portion.

Once all four windows have been completed and are completely dry, they need to be carefully positioned. This means working on the reverse of the card but still producing a correct aspect at the front. If the frames are a bit deep you may not easily be able to position the windows precisely to the sides and bottom cuts in the card. One little trick is to extend the cut-outs with accurately drawn pencil extensions: a few horizontals and verticals will give you added datum lines for the glazing bars. Spread any available UHU type glue all around the cut-out to ensure a good firm fixing, but make sure this is not too blobby or too thick with a risk of it squeezing out on to the window itself. Square it up, press it down,

check it from the front and tweak it, if necessary – then leave it alone. Repeat until all four windows are positioned to your satisfaction and then let the glue harden.

STARTING THE ASSEMBLY

The inside of the shed is almost wholly a matter of individual choice. You can take the route of recreating every detail, real or hypothesized, or you can simply install the area visible through the doorway or glimpsed through the windows. Both options, however, have the same starting point: building the inside platform and vehicle loading bay.

In my experience this is best done with the shed 'box' partly completed. Complete the scored 'V'-shaped incisions and very carefully bend the two gable ends inwards until they are at perfect right angles to the trackside back wall. For safety and rigidity, cut two wall-height lengths from bracing strip, using either balsa or hardwood not less than 5mm square or its triangular equivalent, if you can find any. Squeeze a generous amount of UHU or universal glue into the fold and spread a further thin coat on either side to fix the bracing strip. Depending upon your dexterity both the back corners can be done simultaneously, but keep checking with your square to ensure you've maintained the vital right angle and that the bottom of the three walls remains perfectly horizontal.

Chimney

As can be seen from the photographs and the artwork, the chimney from the small fireplace in the checker's office is built as part of the southwest corner of the shed itself. We therefore only need to complete the remaining two sides and add the decorative capping at the top. The sides are dealt with as a pair of butt-joined pieces with dimensions as necessary to combine with the existing sides to form a perfectly square stack. These are best measured on your own model: they are quite small components and must be a precise fit, and each one may be slightly different. The depth is largely academic as they will be out of sight when beneath the roof. This is another small task for mounting board secured with clear glue.

The capping is quite straightforward and should be made up from two wrappers of 200gsm card or paper. The inner layer is 4mm deep and must finish about 2mm below the top of the stack. The second layer is 2mm deep and is positioned centrally over the first. The shaped capping should be moulded from thin smears of plasticine carefully smoothed and squared with a small palette knife and then painted over with watercolours.

INTERIOR DETAILS

When everything is dry and rigid, with the front or roadside almost like a door ready to be closed, you can now check the exact measurements of the platform itself. At the risk of stating the obvious, these are the full internal lengths of each wall with the corners cut out to fit around the braces.

On a model with a small surface area, such as the Corfe Castle goods shed, the platform should not require any additional strengthening. Mark it on your

remaining card off-cuts and remove it with a scalpel. Take off the corners and slide it into the open box to check the fit. If it does, the next two tasks can be carried out more or less simultaneously.

Decide how you are going to reproduce the wooden planked floor effect on the card platform. This can be simply scored and painted, or you can go the whole way and cut balsa planks to be laid individually. I prefer the second option, using $^3/_{16}$in or even $^1/_4$in strip balsa. Many modellers like to use hardwood strips, but I find them too shiny and dark for a task like this. Shed floors were worn almost white with use and dust. Balsa wood colours get as close as you like to this feel. Balsa is also easy to position and will stay in place quite happily with balsa cement, PVA or universal glue. It is cheap and very easy to cut cleanly with a scalpel. I usually lay them vertically (front to back). Line them up exactly on the edge of the platform and keep them nicely squeezed together to cover the whole area, tidying up any overhanging ends at the front edge. Offer the job up again to check that it fits.

You can now install the eventual fixing points. Cut some short bracing strips from the same material as you used for the corners. Glue the first immediately below the doorway opening on the back wall so that, when the planked platform rests on it, the top of the platform is flush with the bottom of the door opening. Add a couple more on the gable ends at exactly the same height. Then glue a final pair beneath the front of the platform itself, where it will butt onto the roadside wall.

Offer it all up again, this time very carefully closing up the front wall into its final position. Do not glue anything yet. When you are happy you have the positioning right, use a pencil to mark the position of the doorway sides on the platform surface. Once this done you can put the building to one side. We now need to work solely on the platform.

LOADING BAY AND INNER WALLS

Using the doorway opening marks as a datum line, we need to remove a section to allow vehicles and trailers to reverse into a bay for side or end loading.

With the roadside wall acting as a doorway, work out the dimensions needed for the loading dock, put it together, weather it and fix it in place. Don't forget to remove the portion to create the vehicle bay.

Add the remaining pre-assembled chimney sides in the corner, then close and glue the roadside wall. The rigidity provided by the firmly glued loading dock should be adequate but you can add further bracing to the top corners, if necessary.

There is no fixed rule for the depth of this recess: it must be deep enough to give a sensible area for loading, but it must not be so deep that it reduces the area needed for loading and unloading the rail traffic on the other side. Given that the platform is 70mm wide, I would suggest cutting the recess no deeper than 35mm. That still provides sufficient room to barrow load merchandise to and from lorries or waiting railway vans.

Mark and cut it out, taking care not to damage the balsa planks. Once done you can detail the platform to the degree that you want (for the techniques involved, see Chapter 3). I have left the shed empty and just used my usual greyish-white watercolours plus a liberal dusting of talcum powder to render the planked surface.

Carry out another test closing of the remaining side, but again do not yet glue it in place. Instead double-check to see if any of the insides of the three walls are visible through the doorways or windows. You may find it useful to drop the two roof sections in place to create the final viewing conditions.

If the visible walls do need a bit of attention, reopen the front side and get busy with your watercolour paintbrush to give the effect of grubby, whitewashed stone walls. Do not overdo this detailing as hardly anything can be seen.

Now you can glue up the final side, bracing the remaining two corners as before and applying glue to the front of the platform. Close it all up, double-checking cardinal points to ensure it is square, the base is horizontal and the interior platform is level.

One final task at ground level is to fill the sides of the lorry bay below platform level. Here you have a degree of choice, since these 'walls', for want of a better word, could be the same as the exterior, or rubble, random stone or brickwork, old sleepers – or any mix of these. I've also added simple steps so that porters don't have to clamber up onto the platform. You may also note that I've picked out a panel on the back wall and added an old sleeper to protect against enthusiastic lorries reversing. The walls can be measured, cut out and folded off-site, squared up on their subfloor, and then glued beneath the platform edge and to the walls either side of the doorway.

The small subassembly of the walls and floor for the vehicle bay can now be eased into place behind the main entrance. It will need some packing underneath to compensate for the 4mm foundations and to bring the floor up to the correct level.

The interior of the shed roof can barely be seen from any normal angle. If you want to add it, then this is what you should aim to reproduce.

Interior roof detailing on this type of shed is, I would argue, of very little benefit. There are no large entrances for a through track and no roof lights, so it would take a contortionist to see up into the roof space through the windows and doorways. This will be even more pronounced when the door canopies have been modelled. If you must, a few strips of white painted balsa to suggest the roof trusses and cross beams are more than enough.

ROOFS

Having now completed the shell and interior of the shed, it may appear that we could now fix the two roof templates into position, but this must not be done before the rail-side sliding doors have been fitted (see below).

Once that has been done, it is time to consider the best way of covering the roof with slates, chosen from the techniques described for kits in Chapter 3. I would choose a sheet of Superquick D8, which I believe is the

finish most closely resembling the prototype. Some modellers like to cut and stick the slates in overlapping rows, but I can see little benefit in this, especially for all the extra effort and the ever-present risk of misalignment. The project uses the sheet in one piece, but it's your choice. Since this can become a contentious issue, I have included two illustrations of actual slate roofs at normal viewing distance. Whether seen in sunshine or shadow – taken five minutes apart – the individual slates are barely discernible.

The only other point I would make in respect of the roof is the ridge. If you have opted to butt join the two half-templates with no overlap, it is well worthwhile filling the 'V' with a strip of $1/16$in or 2mm balsa or hardwood. This gives the lead flashing or shaped tiles along the ridge a better outline and easier fixing. Lastly don't forget the slight overlap of the tiles beyond the roof templates and the use of discreet barge-boards to disguise the exposed edges of the templates.

Slates are, I think, best left to commercial pre-prints. Their thickness in real life is usually less than ½in (0.17mm to scale) and is barely discernible at any distance. These roofs, less than 50 yards from my window, demonstrate how little detail can be seen.

From here on we are talking about the final phase: detailing. The two canopies over the doorways, however, are quite substantial in their own right. Even the doors will take some time to get them visually correct and, I hope, working.

CANOPIES AND DOORS

Doors

The doors come in pairs and are identical in every respect. This makes them easy to model in one go. As the photographs show, they are substantial items. Each door in the pairs of sliding doors is 5ft (20mm to scale) wide; those on the rail side are 11ft (44mm) tall and on the road side they are 16ft (64mm) tall. They are made of timbers approaching 4in (more than 1mm) in width. It would not be unreasonable to use a standard mounting board as our starting point, although a laminate of two sheets cut from the back of any A4 pad would do the job equally well. A third alternative is to use one sheet of the A4 pad back and plank the front with $^1/_{32}$ balsa strip or hardwood equivalent.

From the modelling viewpoint both pairs are remarkably free of visible ironwork or detailing, so the main task on the mounting board is to cut accurately and score cleanly. By now you should be pretty proficient with a scalpel, so the cutting out is straightforward. Scoring and scribing is only to give a suggestion of the joins between planks and should not be overpronounced. On this occasion we will be using the appropriate 'house colour' of Southern Green enamel instead of the cream of BR days. I suggest the scribing is done either with the back of the scalpel point or with a needle. Avoid tearing, keep the widths accurate and consistent, and above all keep the scribe lines vertical. The lock and doorpull on the road side are the only bits of detail shown in the field photos: add these if you wish and the job is almost done, apart from the engineering.

Making the doors work

The field-visit photograph gives enough detail of the simple engineering that carries these heavy doors to make it fairly easy to reproduce a similar construction in model form. This is certainly a distinct

This view shows the arched entrance from the roadside but also, more importantly, it reveals the very simple mechanism for the sliding doors.

advantage as sliding doors are much easier to make operable than their hinged counterparts, which usually snap their delicate hinges.

For Corfe we preferably need to use metal rods, which are better than plastic (but plastic may be used if there is no alternative). These need to be about 1mm thick and quite stiff: steel is the metal of choice. Each rod needs to be mounted clear of the wall by at least 1mm. The easy option is to use small blocks of balsa at each end, the same cut from mounting board or similar versions from plastic strip. The length of the rod, and hence the positions of the mounting blocks, should be at least 86mm. That is enough to allow the doors to completely overlap the doorways when closed, but draw well clear when open. Cut the rod and glue it at one end securely on to one of the mounting blocks. A dollop of quick-set epoxy completely enveloping the rod will dry quickly and is easy to disguise with a blob of paint.

Turning our attention back to the actual doors, we now need to examine how they might be hung squarely from the rod and remain easy to slide. I tested various paper and thin card loops fixed to the inside of the woodwork but found that none of them were successful. The answer lay in some form of hangers that were fixed into the card itself. In the end I made up four eyelets for each door, using the thinnest available florist's wire looped over a slightly larger plastic rod, and then twisted together to form a shank about 1cm long when cut. Using a small drill in the pin vice, holes were drilled, very carefully, into the top of the door. The two outer ones are about 5mm in from the ends, the other two equidistant in the middle. The eyelet shanks were coated in super glue, pushed into the holes and then quickly threaded onto the waiting rod before the glue hardened. The door now hung squarely and ran easily. All that remained was to epoxy the second mounting block in place. Any extra details were then added and the job put to one side.

Both pairs of doors followed exactly the same procedures, except that the smaller rail-side set is hung from the inside and therefore needs to be installed and checked before the roof is fixed (see above).

The model version also works, which is not so easy when hinges are involved.

Fortunately the only ironwork on the shed doors is the lock and draw-handle. These could easily be suggested by a dab of paint or you could bend some very fine wire and push it into tiny pinholes to make the handle.

Canopies

These sturdy-looking constructions appear to have been added as finishing touches to the building and were not the typical extensions of the main roof. Just to complicate matters, they differ from one another in both size and construction. That need not prevent us from tackling them as a single exercise, as long as we make sure which parts are which.

Once again the main material will be mounting board. This will form the two top roof templates upon which all the other components will be built. The rail-side template measures 64 x 40mm and the road-side template is 60 x 20mm; in both cases one long side joins on to the shed eaves. These dimensions are sufficient to allow for the substantial mouldings that overhang the valences by some 6in all around. It also makes provision for the canopies to 'sit' on the lower parts of the roof by a similar amount.

The easiest method of construction is to work upside down with the roof templates acting as bases. In reality the mouldings would be fixed to the outside of the structure; but since there appears to be a hollow space above the underside or ceiling, we can avoid this intricate bit of modelling and create the mouldings as a series of overlays. These will require some careful cutting out as we need to build three 'steps' in just 6in (2mm to scale). The first layer can be a slightly smaller piece of mounting board cut to slightly less than 1mm all round than the base template. The middle layer is barely discernible and can come from the 200gsm source, again cut just fractionally smaller than the first. The final layer is a further piece of mounting board, smaller again by a similar amount. When all three layers are cut to your satisfaction, test them by eye several times to make sure they align. They can then be laminated together. I would suggest that brushed-on paper glue is the

The two distinctive canopies at Corfe are 'the same but different'. The styles are identical, but the roadside version is smaller than its counterpart protecting the railside operations.

Hold the roof securely and, using the scalpel rather like a wood plane, carve away from yourself.

best option, as this allows a few valuable seconds to adjust the positioning.

Don't rush this exercise and allow each layer to dry properly before fixing the next. If you work on both canopies at the same time it will help to keep the job moving and help you to keep your eye in. It is essential that these subassemblies remain completely flat, so it's worth leaving them overnight beneath a heavy pile of books.

The canopies must fit as horizontal projections commencing approximately four slates up from the edge of the roof. This requires the undersides of the inner faces to be chamfered to match the pitch or slope as closely as possible. Jobs like this are among the most risky of all the scalpel exercises; keep the workpiece upside down, firmly held and always move the blade away from away from you as if you were using a carpenter's plane. Work slowly and, as I frequently advise, keep offering them up to check your progress and avoid being over-enthusiastic and cutting too deeply. When you are satisfied that you've achieved a snug potential fit, turn the canopies right way up and add the tar-felt coating. I find the best

answer is usually the most simple and I cover the roof with strips of masking tape with some brushed-on paper glue to aid adhesion. All that is then needed are thin paper strips for the securing battens and coat of matt black enamel. Now comes the fiddly bit.

Valences

The next step is to fabricate the very distinctive valences: unfortunately, I haven't found a matching version among the many trade offerings. The 200gsm card will look sufficiently solid to capture the character of the original and is an easy material with which to work. The valences are 3ft deep (12mm to scale) and the total length needed will be 244mm. Cut the strip slightly longer to give you space for a few extras. The actual valences are made up of a series of 6in planks, so we must now commence the laborious task of scribing the strip at 2mm intervals. It is vital that these scribe lines are kept vertical and, with more than 100 of them to be done, some form of aid is a good idea. I chose to tape the strip and my thickest ruler to a piece of stout card and the pin-prick all the 2mm divisions. A simple set square

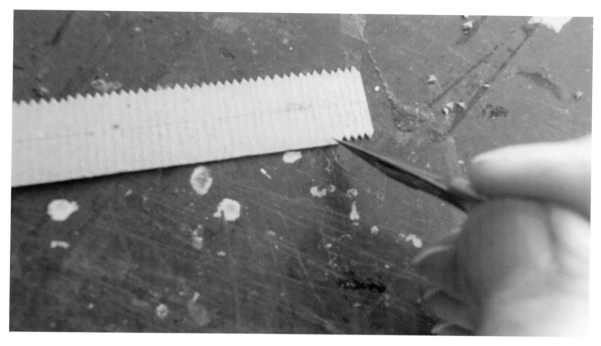

Unfortunately I have been unable to find a correct version of the valences from any trade source. The DIY approach, though, is quite simple, even if it is somewhat tedious. It is little more than nicking out a series of small V-shaped cuts from strips of thin 200gsm card. You need to be patient as you need about 250mm of it.

was then held against the ruler and slid along as each plank was scribed.

The task is now to cut the 'V' shape at the bottom of each plank. Keep the workpiece taped down and, to ensure accuracy and consistency, repeat the 2mm pin-pricks, this time starting from halfway in on the first plank. These marks will be the points of the 'V' cuts you now need to make. Finally draw a fine line 1mm up from the bottom of the strip to give the correct depth to the cuts. You will now need a scalpel with a new blade, so be careful when nicking the strip in a series of angled cuts from the scribed planks to the pin-pricks.

When you have completed enough for all six sides, separate them from the strip and pencil an identifier on the back before putting them to one side. This may seem tiresome, but it does limit the risk of damage or distortion.

With all six portions ready for installation, attention can now be given to the question of how to fit them to the undersides of the two roof assemblies.

The neatest way is to glue reinforcing strips of square-section balsa just inside all three sides. Positioning is critical, since you need to be able to secure the valences to them while still leaving a correct amount of the overhanging 'moulding' exposed. To attempt to give an exact measurement would be risky; the best solution is to take two strips of 200gsm card, align the outer surface with the edge of the moulding and glue the balsa alongside the inner surface. The correct lengths of valence can themselves now be glued in place. If in doubt check the research photographs.

Canopy details

There is little need for any detailing to the undersides as they remain largely unseen in normal viewing conditions. You may want to model the supporting brackets on the rail side, in which case just use the image as a guide. The supporting trusses are an easier option and a few thin strips of mounting board are quite sufficient to represent these.

The underside of the canopy on the railside contains some fairly substantial woodwork as well as cast-iron brackets. Most of this will remain unseen, but this is what it looks like.

A few card strips are probably all that is needed to suggest the woodwork and the cast-iron supports.

The very last item is the decorative strip of wood-work that runs around both the canopies, about a foot above the bottom. The thinnest piece of balsa, hardwood or even plastic strip will do, but paint it before fixing. The canopies will always be vulnerable items; delay installing them until after all the final detailing like soffits, barge-boards and ironwork has been completed.

CONCLUSIONS

This particular project was intended to be both a test vehicle for design, assembly and finishes, as well as a subject for your own modelling. In short, it was part instructional and part inspirational. It should be well within the scope of a first-time scratch-builder and yet still prove to be an attractive prototype for those with more advanced skills. It is a typical example of this type of small shed and, by localising the actual style of the finish, it could be easily re-regionalized anywhere in the country.

I should finally declare my choice between the various finishes for the shed. I would definitely opt for the very simple, but very effective, 'poly-plate and pencil'. It was relatively quick, it was certainly cheap and easy to source, and it was fairly straight-forward to execute. The actual stonework on the Swanage branch is quite difficult to replicate and is certainly not available as an off-the-shelf aid. In my view this preferred method gets close to the real thing, with the proviso that the colour and degree of relief modelled are somewhat subjective. In my defence, however, should you be able to visit this popular line on a regular basis, you will doubtless find that its perceived colours and textures look different on each occasion.

ABOVE AND OVERLEAF: *The finished model should make an attractive addition to any goods yard, especially when your own version will have all its walls done in the same chosen finish, unlike this project example. Although the shed looks properly Southern and distinctly Purbeck, simply changing the finish would enable you to resite it anywhere in the country.*

CHAPTER SEVEN

CONCLUSIONS, SOURCES AND FURTHER READING

We have now covered just about every aspect of modelling steam-era goods facilities and workings. I hope that it has given some insight into the importance of goods operations as well as some suggestions about how these might be best replicated on your own models. The goods train should never be reduced to a few shiny wagons trundling around in any gaps between passenger workings. Nor should the goods yard be tucked into a left-over corner on the layout to serve a shiny cardboard shed and a cattle-pen full of equally shiny Friesians. The trains and yards both offer tremendous opportunities to the imaginative modeller in pursuit of railway-like images and prototypical operations. The current ranges of r-t-r goods and mixed traffic locomotives and rolling stock can provide everything one needs, while a browse around the auction sites, kit manufacturers and toy sales often yields the more unusual items to add to the fleet.

A well-planned yard is a source of endless fun to those who enjoy realistic shunting moves. Equally, a well-modelled yard is a visual asset on any layout and provides a wealth of detailing and cameos that one can enjoy while the expresses are going round. The entire freight sector, to use modern parlance, is a modeller's paradise. It is almost the case that one simply cannot have enough wagons: with more than 450 on my fleet, I am still adding more and 'improving' those that I have. They stimulate the enthusiasm for weathering, rebranding with excellent transfers, improving the wheel-sets, standardizing couplings and adding extra details and authentic loads. The choice of motive power is also full of scope for those who enjoy some fettling in front of the television.

The selection of locos is almost as wide as one's pocket is deep. All manner of engines could be rostered on to almost every type of goods train. The only exception is that you mustn't roster a non-vacuum type, like a ROD, WD, or 04, on a fast-fitted working: but the reverse is quite acceptable. Even in our early 1950s 'golden era' many a harassed running-foreman had to shove a Hall, V2 or Arthur on to the plodding, loose-coupled coal empties. Excellent though today's r-t-r engines undoubtedly are, they can still benefit from some skilful weathering, etched plates, correct lamp codes, real coal on the tender, storm sheets, fire irons – and, above all, by a crew that look like proper enginemen, perhaps accompanied by an inspector or pilotman to keep an eye on things. As for the brake van: the guard might be seen on the veranda, the type and size of van should be appropriate to the train weight, and don't forget the three tail lamps.

Lastly, it's a great area to research, which is a rather fancy way to describe simply sitting back with your favourite albums, DVDs, magazines or anecdotes and soaking up the atmosphere. Always remember to look beyond the main subject and study what is going on in the background. The goods yard or a 'mixed' on the relief may not be as glamorous as the speeding express, but who knows what interesting details you might spot in the background. A classic example can be found in the illustrations in Chapter 5: the photographer may have been concentrating his efforts on the main line, but he unwittingly contributed much to the very scarce archive on Moreton Yard.

We have progressed, step by step and blow by blow, from exploring our main subjects and opening the wrapping on our first kit, right through to scratch building and the major test-project of constructing a complete yard. We have even looked at ways of improving our rolling-stock and keeping the whole thing truly 'railway-like' and original, not just another cloned and shop-bought model railway. In short, I hope we have come to be real railway modellers. I have certainly re-learned some vital lessons that I had lost over the passing decades, so my modelling, too, will be the better thanks to this journey.

SOURCES

Throughout the book I have tried to concentrate on materials, tools, kits and accessories that are the most widely available across the country. However, I do acknowledge that some outlets that are household names in one area may be totally unknown in another, so you may have to do some research to find their equivalents.

Kits and bits: Always start by checking out local model shop and the nearest toy fairs or exhibitions. Next in line come the advertisers in the model press and the numerous internet sources. Finally, for second-hand items, try local auctioneers or take a chance on the bigger specialist houses.

Tools and materials: These are always best purchased locally across the counter so you can test or examine what you are buying. In many cases specialist items can come from model shops, while more general offerings can be found in many 'pound shops', DIY stores or outlets like Range, Hobbycraft or In-Excess. Discount art shops are also worth a visit. The web may be another avenue, as much as a means of discovering something new as for a source of supply.

Models: If you want to buy new then your local dealership must take priority. If, however, you enjoy the potential challenges offered by second-, third- or fourth-hand, then toy fairs and auctions are a must. At a pinch even car boot sales can produce surprises.

FURTHER READING

One can never have a big enough library of books on railway modelling and related subjects, so please view the list below as a starting point only. Some of these books are out-of-print, but most specialist second-hand bookshops should be able to find them.

Arlett, Mike and Lockett, David, *Great Western Steam 1934–1949* (Lightmoor Press) ISBN 978 1 899889 46 4

Arlett, Mike and Lockett, David, *Western Region Steam 1950–1965* (Lightmoor Press) ISBN 978 1 899889 60 0

Bardsley, Richard, *Making a Start in N Gauge Railway Modelling* (Crowood), ISBN 978 1 84797 556 0

Barlow, Bernard, *Didcot Engineman* (Wild Swan), ISBN 978 1 874103 20 2

Drayton, John, *On the Footplate: Memories of a GWR Engineman* (Bradford Barton) ISBN 978 0 85153 299 8

Essery, Bob, *Freight Train Operation for the Railway Modeller* (Ian Allan), ISBN 978 0 71103 142 5

Essery, Bob, *Railway Operation for the Modeller* (Midland Publishing Ltd), ISBN 978 1 85780 168 2

Essery, Bob, *Shunting and Marshalling* (Ian Allan), ISBN 978 0 71103 632 1

Gasson, Harold, *Firing Days: Reminiscences of a Great Western Fireman* (Oxford Publishing Company) ISBN 978 0 902888 25 8

Gasson, Harold, *Footplate Days: More Reminiscences of a Great Western Fireman* (Oxford Publishing Company) ISBN 978 0 902888 51 7

Gwilliam, Ray, *A Loco Fireman Looks Back* (Bradford Barton) ISBN 978 0 85153 349 0

Hands, P.B., *British Railways Steam Hauled Freight Trains (Vol 1)* (Defiant Publications) 978 0 94685742 5

Jenkinson, David, *Historical Railway Modelling* (Pendragon), ISBN 978 1 89981 610 1

Kelsey Media, *Moving The Goods (1) Serving the Community* (bookzine exclusive to WH Smith), ISBN 978 1 909786 52 3

Kelsey Media, *Moving The Goods (3) Coal* (Kelsey Media) (bookzine exclusive to WH Smith), ISBN 978 1 909786 58 5

Marriott, Peter, *Railway Modelling Skills* (Crowood), ISBN 978 1 84797 955 1

McMillan, Andy, *Making Model Railway Buildings* (Crowood), ISBN 978 1 84797 340 5

Toton Engineman: The Autobiography of a Railwayman (Steam World) ISBN 978 0 9927 398 0 5

Wright, David, *Making Urban Buildings for Model Railways* (Crowood), ISBN 978 1 84797 568 3

INDEX